PRAISE FOR THE ADVE
THE HONEY BAD

Winger and wordsmith Nick Cummins can now
add author to his resume.
The Project, Network Ten

It's been a very long time since I've laughed
so much at a book.
Goodreads

Tales of the Honey Badger is Australian yarn-telling
at its modern finest. It's larger than life, and yet somehow
captures perfectly the mischievous childhoods
many of us remember fondly.
Hush Hush Biz

Hilarious. Cummins recounts adventures, mishaps
and momentous occasions in the most colloquially
articulate (is that even possible?) of ways.
He had me in stitches throughout.
Goodreads

PRAISE FOR THE ADVENTURES OF THE HONEY BADGER

ADVENTURES
OF THE
HONEY BADGER

First published in Australia in 2016
by HarperCollinsPublishers Australia Pty Limited
ABN 36 009 913 517
harpercollins.com.au

HarperCollins*Publishers*
Level 13, 201 Elizabeth Street, Sydney, NSW 2000, Australia
Unit D1, 63 Apollo Drive, Rosedale, Auckland 0632, New Zealand
A 53, Sector 57, Noida, UP, India
1 London Bridge Street, London, SE1 9GF, United Kingdom
2 Bloor Street East, 20th floor, Toronto, Ontario M4W 1A8, Canada
195 Broadway, New York, NY 10007

National Library of Australia Cataloguing-in-Publication data:

Cummins, Nick, 1987- author.
Adventures of the Honey Badger / Nick Cummins, Mark Cummins.
978 0 7333 3786 4 (paperback)
978 1 4607 0774 6 (ebook)
Subjects: Cummins, Nick, 1987–Anecdotes.
Cummins, Nick, 1987–Humour.
Rugby Union football players–Australia–Humour.
Australian wit and humour.
Other Creators/Contributors: Cummins, Mark, author.
796.333092

Cover and internal design by Hazel Lam, HarperCollins Design Studio
Cover images: Main photo of Nick Cummins by Darren Holt; all other photos of Nick Cummins courtesy of the author; background images by shutterstock.com
Typeset in Minion Pro by HarperCollins Design Studio
Printed and bound in Australia by Griffin Press
The papers used by HarperCollins in the manufacture of this book are natural, recyclable product made from wood grown in sustainable plantation forests. The fibre source and manufacturing processes meet recognised international environmental standards, and carry certification.

NICK CUMMINS

with a bit of help from my old man, MARK CUMMINS

Dedication

Life is a wonderful thing. Sometimes when I'm alone on a beach or some other special place, I think about what's ahead and where I've been. It's not easy, and for some almost too hard.

Don't judge or be too quick to criticise because we all have our goods and bads.

Be the light in someone's distance, say the word that brings the smile. Be the rock in the pond that spreads the ripple of happiness far and wide.

I haven't led a privileged life. My family has felt joy and pain like all families. We've learnt to choose life, to press forward, full speed ahead and damn the torpedoes. Don't take anything too seriously because there's far too much fun to be had.

I dedicate this book to the goers in life, the people who will not be beaten, who get back up, dust off and choose laughter as the best option.

Love much

Nick (and Mark)

Dedication

CONTENTS

Welcome to the...

HOW TO RESPOND TO A FART:

'A bit more choke and you would have started'

ON WHITE WATER RAFTING

(And the importance of staying in the boat)

I've been rafting a few times over the years and it's a real buzz. The first time I went I was about 12 – the perfect roll of the dice.

Dad, my two older brothers Luke and Nathan, along with a couple of the old boy's mates and their sons joined us on what would become an epic adventure in northern NSW.

Our mission? To tear the heart out of the Nymboida River and take the rafting world to a whole new level.

So we packed ourselves into the Tarago van – remembering I've got enough siblings to fill an entire Sevens roster – and roared down the Pacific Highway, full of hope and wonder.

The trip was going to take a few hours, so the old man brought along a Viking hat complete with horns. Anyone who said something stupid or cracked a poor joke had to wear it – in and out of the van. Because of the average IQ of the travelling party, the hat changed owners many a time, and yours truly was a frequent recipient.

Anyhow, the hat had been making the rounds with the noticeable omission of Dad's mate, Steve, who was either highly intelligent or painfully unfunny. So finally, having had enough of missing out, he made a formal request to don the hat and placed it on his melon. I was more confused than an All Black at a bookstore. So I asked him why exactly he wanted it, given he hadn't said anything. He replied, 'I had a stupid thought.' Now, that's integrity!

A few hours later we were hooning down the Nymboida River in two rafts at a rate of knots and absolutely thrilled. Then we heard the roar of the rapids and there were some concerned looks.

I WAS MORE CONFUSED THAN AN ALL BLACK AT A BOOKSTORE.

We had all the safety gear. And like a first-timer on the alpine slopes looking to impress, we *looked* like we knew what we were doing. But at the very last corner before the rapids, elation made way for unadulterated adrenalin as the roar of the pumping water grew ever louder and our rafting guide (the bloke at the back) stressed that this was an extremely difficult task and that we had to hang on for our lives.

We approached the rapids at a fair pace and came to a 45-degree rock ledge, we were full of confidence! So much so that halfway down my brothers and I jumped up and dropped our strides, mooning the other rafters. But unbeknown to us, the rapids had barely started.

Between the noise of the rapids, the screams of the moonies and the yelling of the old man telling us to sit the hell down, it was pure and utter chaos! Then it happened.

We hit the bottom of the rapids and the rafts became airborne. What a bloody buzz!

After a verbal serve from the raft captain, who could best be described as filthy, he told us the next rapid was too dangerous and that he'd take the rafts down alone while we legged it. Apparently, a few punters had pulled the pin in that section of the river and we'd hardly impressed our instructor with our professionalism.

The walk was no easy task either. We had to climb a rocky outcrop about 10–15 metres high before we reached a ledge and were instructed to jump off and float down the river. We didn't need to be told twice.

One at a time, the boys made the leap of faith, hootin' and hollerin' until they slammed into the deep aqua below. Finally, it was only myself and one of Dad's mates left – not Steve, that smart bastard was cluey enough to wait for the water to be broken by one of my brothers before making his descent like a pin. Ten out of ten for form.

This poor bugger, Chris, was once a good athlete but because of a couple of knee replacements had no push power for the jump. He just leant forward and said to me, 'Push me, you bastard!'

A BIG MISTAKE:

1. Balls-up
2. Blue

A LOOK AROUND AND PEE:

A fox's breakfast

Yes, sir! I gave him a good taste of the old Cummins' squirrel grip and suitcased him right off the edge. I remember his descent in fine detail – it was like watching a YouTube 'biggest fails' video, Chris was falling like a cartoon character in a bad dream before hitting the water like someone whose parachute hadn't opened. I thought I'd killed him! Suffice to say, I let out a heavy sigh of relief when finally his life jacket brought him to the surface. He looked liked he'd landed face-first, his face was about as red as my cheeks were about to be when my old man yelled out, 'Don't kill the bastard, he's my accountant!'

I GAVE HIM A GOOD TASTE OF THE OLD CUMMINS' SQUIRREL GRIP AND SUITCASED HIM RIGHT OFF THE EDGE

I now realise how important these people are in your life. I don't think Dad's paid tax since '92.

Moving on, we floated down to meet the rafts, about a kilometre downstream. It was anything but relaxing, as we were flung around like pinballs from one rock formation to the other. It'd been at least an hour by now, so it was time for some grub. We pulled up for lunch and strapped the feed bag on. The tucker was good and as the old fellas lay back they had that 'I need a beer' look screaming from every pore. To achieve Dad's final ambition, it was clear we had to clean up this last rapid like the professionals we thought we were.

We climbed into our rafts like clowns into a punch buggy. Before my raft had even pushed off we watched in hysterics as

Dad's raft went arse over head just 30 seconds after the mighty quest began. The old blokes looked like a group of giant spiders trying to claw their way up the toilet bowl before it flushed.

Dad reckoned he stared death in the face and was on the brink of drowning before by some stroke of luck he was presented with something to push off against, and launched himself to the surface. Turns out that something was Chris, who breached the water a few seconds later like a harpooned sperm whale, coughing, spluttering and gagging. He blew up that someone had stood on his head and pushed off him. The old boy made a vocal stand right there and then that he wouldn't have a beer again until he caught the culprit. He didn't have the heart to tell him the truth. Nor the willpower to go any longer without a beer. Mission complete.

THE OLD BLOKES LOOKED LIKE A GROUP OF GIANT SPIDERS TRYING TO CLAW THEIR WAY UP THE TOILET BOWL BEFORE IT FLUSHED.

THE MASSAGE INCIDENT

(Try not to put your foot in it)

Other than a meat pie, a cold one and the touch of a fine woman, there's nothing better than a good massage. Especially if the latter is being performed by said woman.

Over the years playing footy I've had thousands of 'em – massages that is – and afterwards you always feel like an absolute superhero, even if you're slipperier than an eel in an olive jar. Well, I was home on a break and looking forward to a bit of surfing and fishing. But I wasn't about to give up my weekly ritual – even if it was out of my loot and not the ARU's. So one morning I put it on the old boy that we slip up for a massage and he was surprisingly cool about it, given he's normally pretty conservative about most things. He still refuses to use chopsticks – adamant the Japanese of all people know better than to stick with obsolete technology. The fork won. It's a no contest. You won't see anyone – except hipsters – wearing a Walkman over an iPod.

Anyhow, the old boy was agreeable to a rubdown on the condition his masseuse was a woman – because he didn't want a bloke slaving all over him. Personally, I reckon he'd been watching too many movies about Turkish prisons and gladiators, but off we went.

The setup was standard. We were in these cubicles side-by-side and we had to wear these disposable grundies – or mosquito nets – for the old tackle. I'd just started to nod off when I heard a blood-curdling scream from the old man's cubicle. Followed directly by a thud!

PERSONALLY, I RECKON HE'D BEEN WATCHING TOO MANY MOVIES ABOUT TURKISH PRISONS AND GLADIATORS.

My first concern was that he might have got carried away and been belted one. But then the truth emerged. The poor girl was walking on the old boy's back while hanging onto the tops of the partition and misjudged her step while working on the coight region – and I don't mean she missed the table.

Now, I'm OK with most things, but when you drop the heel into the sprocket you know that carnage is about to follow. Ask any rugby league player. She was far from a big girl, a scale model compared to Dad, and her leg must have disappeared up to her knee.

I'm sure she felt she had been swallowed by a groper and then whacked over the head with one when she hit the deck. Her leg broke free from the vortex of the great beast's nether regions. The suction release alone sounded like a cork popping. Her screams of terror brought people from everywhere. You'd think his unusually hairy back would have provided some sort of traction …

THE OLD BLOKE WAS TRYING TO CONSOLE HER AND GET HIS KIT ON AT THE SAME TIME AND IT LOOKED SUS!

By the time I made it in there the old bloke was trying to console her and get his kit on at the same time and it looked sus! How else could it look?

After explaining my name was Drew Mitchell and the old boy was the Australian Wallabies coach, we paid up and fled the scene at Olympic-winning speed, leaving a one-legged masseur to recount the story of how she was swallowed alive and lived to tell the tale.

I'm told she never oiled another back again. Won't even cook with the stuff.

NOSE:

1. Cherry picker
2. Beak
3. Honker
4. Sniffer

OBVIOUS:

Stands out like a dog's clackers

FEAR AND LOATHING IN BOSNIA

What's that you say? Is there such an animal as rugby in Norway? Oh yeah.

For about 30 years, apparently, Norway has had a national rugby team, which has had its ups and downs. Most of the teams have their fair share of expats and local Vikings, and some years ago my brother Nathan opted to follow a good sort to Stavanger – a small city on the southwest coast – and was pleasantly surprised to find a comp to play in.

Now, Nath was always a pretty handy rugby player and had won premierships all over the joint. So when he asked my opinion, there was nothing to say but 'go for it!' It'd be a bloody good story at the very least.

Once he arrived he hooked up with Stavanger Rugby Club, a small mob that had been doing it a little tough compared to their big cousins Oslo and Bergen. And like the champion he is – and possibly aided by the fact he couldn't understand their appeals for him not to – it wasn't long before Nath took over the joint, becoming captain-coach of the club and national side. Yep, Norway's eligibility rules are looser than Queensland's in State of Origin.

Of course, he was met with some trepidation and solid resistance from some of the old rugby heads who didn't believe Nathan could do much to help the joint. So one night, after a few refreshments at the local, Nathan proclaimed that Stavanger would go the full year undefeated. Brave or stupid? In this context, they meant the same thing.

NORWAY'S ELIGIBILITY RULES ARE LOOSER THAN QUEENSLAND'S IN STATE OF ORIGIN.

This was met with a raucous chorus of laughter. Tom Ward, a former rugby player, suggested he would walk around the harbour nude if Nath's proclamation rang true.

Well, that was incentive enough for Nath, who's spent a lifetime ensuring his best and closest are oft humiliated. And sure enough, Stavanger won the 2014 national grand final – undefeated. Nath had come good on his word so old Tommy did the same – not to the same amount of applause, mind you – and paraded his manhood along the wharves for all and sundry to view in absolute horror.

Rugby's typically a winter sport, so it was quite cold on that Norwegian morning, and the conditions did little to exaggerate Tom's assets. To add to this evening of merriment and likely as a result, Tom had become newly single and ensured little chance of immediate change to his status. Poor bastard claimed he was batting above anyway and this was the last straw – figuratively and literally.

I'm glad to say, Stavanger has now won Sevens and 15s national titles undefeated the past two years. They should drug test the bastards! Especially Nathan.

But it hasn't been all glamour for Nath. His first game for the national side as captain was against Bosnia – in Bosnia!

IF YOU DIDN'T HAVE BULLET HOLES IN YOUR HOUSE YOU WEREN'T HAVING A GO.

It was a little town named Zenica and is what the crew on *The Block* would describe as a real fixer-upper. To be clear, that's what they would say. I'm not that insensitive. But if you didn't have bullet holes in your house you weren't having a go.

The stadium wasn't much different, but thankfully there was some safety signage out front – 'No dogs & no guns'.

The Norwegians warmed up to the jeers of the crowd, marching music and dogs howling at the flares and crackers, which were all the go. Like Nath, the referee obviously wanted to get out of town alive, and appeased the locals with some interesting decisions. It was rugby at its best – the linesman puts his flag up for illegal play, the crowd threatens him with guns and dogs, and the linesman lowers his flag. Pretty straightforward stuff and from a player's perspective on the home side, the home crowd really is an advantage. Maybe that's where the saying comes from?

THE BOYS HAD THEIR HORNS POINTING FORWARD AND ALL SIGNS POINTED TOWARDS A BIG NIGHT.

Anyway, the boys got done at the death – no pun intended – by a few points and they were pretty down about it. Enter the old man and a very patient mate of his, Russ, who forced their way into the dressing room. Russ distributed the beers while the old fella climbed onto the table – for the first time since the massage incident – and commanded the attention of the crowd like the rugby god he believes he is.

Better yet, the door was shut and he had a captive audience. I'm told the pep talk went something like this: 'Gentleman, today you played your hearts out for Norway and you are Norway's finest. Tomorrow, they'll still be Bosnians!' The dressing room erupted and Norway was back on track.

The following week, Norway hammered Bulgaria 42–0 at home. The boys had their horns pointing forward and all signs pointed towards a big night.

A few of the troops wandered down to the harbour for a bit

of stomach lining before the celebrations. Nath, Dad, Russ and myself were having a feed when two middle-aged English tourists turned up asking the question, 'What are you having?' Dad was quick to exclaim: 'He's having the whale, but it's a bit tough. I'm really into this dolphin. It's tender as, on account of it being clubbed to death.' You should have seen the look on our faces let alone the tourists' as they retreated in horror. We've since had Dad undergo a psych eval and are awaiting the results.

Note: No dolphins or whales were hurt during this shit-talk.

HOW TO DESCRIBE A DOPEY BASTARD:

'If brains were dynamite, he couldn't blow up a letterbox' or 'He hasn't got enough brains to give himself a headache' or 'You can't put brains in a monument'

LATE-NIGHT DEATH THREATS

It was 2011 and the Western Force was on tour to South Africa. We landed in Johannesburg, one of the finer cities, then bussed it to Durban – also a city.

After making the hotel regret putting in an all-you-can-eat buffet for breakfast, we headed for training at a field previously scoped out by team staff and deemed to be a secure location, safe from the peering eyes of the opposition team's undercover staff.

All seemed to be going pretty well until the end of the session when one of the lads having a shot at goal kicked the ball right over the fence and into some long grass.

I drew the short straw and had to go collect the thing. As I stepped over the wire fence, I copped an almighty shock – some bloke pops up from the grass with a long-lens camera, grabs his tripod and bolts deeper into the scrub.

OUR SECURITY GUARD TOOK OFF AFTER HIM LIKE HE'D JUST SPOTTED ELVIS

He was moving well for a big fella. And with high knee lifts like that I had to make a decision fast – either engage in hot pursuit or alert our security (ex Special Forces) to cut him off on the other side of the scrub. Finally, my moment had come. A moment I'd trained my whole life for, to take down a wildebeest with my bare hands at speed. Or be badly hurt trying.

As much as I love the thrill of the chase – hence why I don't bat an eye at being knocked back by a woman, it lets me enjoy that thrill all over again – I decided against it and let common sense prevail. Largely on account of the fact that it's very common for people to carry concealed guns in these parts – either holstered on the ankle or the hip. And it would have been extremely difficult to play that weekend with half me guts missing.

While I might have pulled the pin, the spy's troubles were only just beginning. Our security guard took off after him like he'd just spotted Elvis and spent the next couple of hours scouring the bush in hot pursuit. But to no avail.

That night I asked the security guard what he'd have done if old mate pulled a gun on him. The bloke turns to me and says:

'I'm a walking f*&king weapon station!' With the rugby gods as my witness, he wasn't joking. I was never great at maths, but I think I counted four guns, ammo and two knives.

Assured my life was in safe hands, I polished off my meal – and his – and headed to my room to catch some Zs in the fart sack. I'd just dutch-ovened myself for a third time when the phone rang: 'Honey Badger, I'm going to kill you,' says a deep South African voice. At first I thought it may have been a former scorned lover so I kept my response to a polite 'mmmm'. Then came: 'Then, I'm going to eat you.' I quickly discovered that not only was it for sure a male voice, ruling out the earlier scenario, but it was no joke. Remembering there are more guns than people in these parts, and with the game coming up in a few days, I didn't want to stir things up. But he kept ringing. As many as eight times a night for three nights in a row, and his message remained largely the same – that his team was going to beat us and that he was personally going to kill and eat me. Didn't he know how tough this battered body would be?

'HONEY BADGER, I'M GOING TO KILL YOU,' SAYS A DEEP SOUTH AFRICAN VOICE.

Anyhow, the game finally came around and we got smoked like tofu at a vegan pride parade. They knew everything we were doing, they were in the spots where we were gonna be well before us and shut down our every move – line-outs, scrums, everything. It was like they knew our plans ...

I think they put 40–50 points on us, and turns out the bloke on the phone was half right – they did beat us, but I've yet to be eaten.

Termite problem? I'll fix it.

OUT OF PLACE:
A pickpocket at a nudist camp

BAKED BEANS:
Fart fodder

AN INTERESTING DRUG TEST

(Or easy 90 millilitre)

It was 2008 at the Western Force and the most dreaded time of the year for any athlete – pre-season. In the guts of summer and with temps in the early 40s, a two-and-a-half-hour on-field training session is enough to leave you as dry as a dead dingo's donger.

Just when you thought it couldn't get any worse comes the cry from one of the boys – 'The ball-starers are here!' And as we leave the field come three blokes and a woman in matching uniforms.

Now, being fairly new to the game, I was unfamiliar with the term 'ball-starer', which I had only heard a week earlier when in the showers. Team-mates would refer to good old Sam Wykes as a 'ball-starer', largely because Sam would be the first in the showers and the last to leave and say such things as 'I got ya' – some sort of sick comparison in appendage sizes and insinuating he had some sort of advantage. Truth was, he'd just stay in the showers long enough until he finally got 'a win'.

'YA GOTTA HAVE A SNAKE'S HISS IMMEDIATELY AFTER IMPACT. IT'S SCIENCE.'

Anyhow, with Wykesy nowhere in sight, I had no idea why the 'ball-starer' call was being thrown around. But as the team left the field, Ryan Cross, Drew Mitchell and myself were randomly selected for drug testing by the four perfectly matching enforcers of the anti-doping authority.

Now, I've got no issue with keeping the game clean. But after that sort of session, you're pretty dry from your mouth on down. Morale was pretty low, us thinking we could be in for a long haul. So we chugged back as much water as possible to speed things up but after 90 minutes there was still nothing. Then boom! I had an idea. I turned to the boys: 'What if I drop a Richard the Third, 'cause ya gotta have a snake's hiss immediately after impact. It's science.' The lads just laughed at me but I wasn't about to be deterred. So I alerted the tester, who happened to be the woman, that 'I'm ready to have a crack'.

She warned that if my sample didn't meet the 90 ml requirement I'd have to start the whole process all over again. So I put her doubts to bed, or enhanced them depending on which way you look at it, with a quick proverb: 'Fortune favours the brave.' And with that, I pressed forward to the throne.

She follows suit, somewhat confused by my unsheathed seating position on the bogger. 'I'm sorry, mate, but there's something I gotta do.' Her eyes squinted and her forehead crinkled, an immediate sign that she understood just what my intentions were.

You see, the rules state that the urine must be seen leaving the body, meaning the sample takers have to get a full view of your setup. From where this lady was standing, the view would have been dreadful – a close-up of a waterfall with a mud slide in the background. It was a flurry of activity and none of it pretty. And after a few seconds that must have felt like hours, success! I hit 95 ml and emptied the tank – and I worked for every drop. A proud achievement in the face of adversity. And, well, the face of a poor inspector who is still having therapy.

FROM WHERE THIS LADY WAS STANDING, THE VIEW WOULD HAVE BEEN DREADFUL

She didn't seem to share my excitement as we exited the crime scene. As we came outside the boys took one look at her and said, 'Poor thing.' To which I replied, 'Could have been worse though. The roles could have been reversed.'

That's the day I fully understood the term 'ball-starer'.

HAS THE ARSE HANGING OUT OF HIS STRIDES:

Broke

HAIR LIKE A BUSH PIG'S ARSE

Messy

SOME FISHY BUSINESS UP NORTH

The coast of WA has always been a magical place for me. Like the old man's shed, there's something almost ancient about the joint. You know, vibe-wise. The beaches and the desert landscape seem to go on forever.

There's a lot of history along the West Oz shores, some inspiring and some exceptionally tragic. Like the book by Peter FitzSimons, which I read all by myself, about the shipwreck of the *Batavia* – some of the buggers got really carried away and were later hung by the rescuers. Just when they thought being shipwrecked was the worst thing to happen to them that week …

Anyhow, my memories of the joint aren't as savage. In fact, quite the opposite. Because, whenever you've got a fishing rod in one hand and an ice cold stubbie in the other, there's no such thing as a bad time. Especially at a little place called Quobba Station.

Quobba Station is located on the bottom tip of Ningaloo Reef Marine Park, covers about 80 clicks of coastline, and the fishing, snorkelling and surfing are top-notch. Add a brewery and a 24/7 butcher and the place would be heaven on earth. Come to think of it, I might look into that.

The accommodation is pretty flash, too. The humpies, shacks, huts and luxury eco tents on the Red Bluff cliffs are deadset better than my apartment. Which admittedly, isn't difficult. I've been told I have the housekeeping skills of a mongrel goat. Despite that reputation, the owners, Tim and Sarah Meecham, were only too happy to welcome me and my ragtag bunch of mates.

I'VE BEEN TOLD I HAVE THE HOUSEKEEPING SKILLS OF A MONGREL GOAT.

I'd planned this tour to coincide with a bye weekend in the rugby, so after our game against the Bulls I ripped straight home and prepared for a 4am leave.

Better yet, the lads at Sweden's finest automaker had lent me some wheels and we scored a heap of rods and lures. Finally, I could lose a handful of lures and not have to shell out a month's wages to get back in the water.

Now, believe it or not, my company included my brother Luke, good mate Blair and the old man – can't seem to shake the bloke. Suffice to say, I was pretty pumped. The fish didn't stand a chance and we knew it.

IT WAS LIKE A DUTCH OVEN IN A SARDINE TIN.

At around 4.30am we took our starting positions – the old boy as co-pilot and the troops in the back. The car was chock a block and the boys in the back weren't just struggling for leg space but air, too. It was like a dutch oven in a sardine tin. But I had plenty of room, so all was cool.

We had an 11-hour drive ahead of us and you have to be pretty careful driving before dawn along the desert road – roos, wallabies and various other creatures with a death-wish come charging out at the last minute to test out the bull bar. I can only assume it's peer pressure from their mates. Why the hell would you play chicken with a car?

After a few stops for refreshments and grub, we finally made it to Quobba and prepared ourselves for battle the next day.

Now, fishing up there is not your standard issue. You need to climb down a steep rocky slope to get to the rock platform of your choice. It's a bit of a mission but once you're there it's happy days. And within seconds, yours truly was on! First cast, too!

It was a big Spanish mackerel and by the way it was fighting, I could only assume it was on whatever Lance Armstrong flushed down the dunny before the USADA kicked in his door.

It pulled about 300 metres of line and when it slowed after its first run I thought I had him and took the foot off the gas.

Then, suddenly, he roared back towards the shore and it was one helluva job keeping the line tight. Was he coming for me? I'd never had a fish come at me before, so I was baffled. Until Blair screamed the one word no fisherman, or life-loving human for that matter, wants to hear: 'Shark!'

He'd spotted a four-metre bronze whaler on the hunt and by the looks of him, it was no surprise he was encouraging some extra speed out of the mackerel. In our direction, no less.

I'm sure the shark felt he had a greater need for the fish than I did.

I did my best to save that mackerel from the jaws of the apex predator – in an effort to feed myself, of course – but 20 metres from the platform it was all over. My one-metre mackerel became a head and a few gizzards. It was the ocean equivalent of being face-palmed by Sonny Bill Williams.

But that was just the start of it. Every bloody cast some big bastard with a fin and a lot of teeth made those fish swim faster and then had them for lunch. We must have hooked up on at least 20 occasions but every time they were snaked by a Noah. It was my high school dance all over again, the big dogs coming in to swoop away the prize I'd worked so hard to get.

I SAW THIS MONSTER, MY NEMESIS, LURKING NEAR THE ROCK SHELF.

Finally, I decided to fight fire with fire. I saw this monster, my nemesis, lurking near the rock shelf. No doubt he was hoping one of us would fall in. And I'd considered giving the old man a shove as a distraction to give me a shot at reeling in a mackerel untouched.

Alas, I baited up the hook with a small reef fish carcass, threw a good cast and bang! It was on – with a four-metre bronze whaler with a set of teeth only a dentist could love.

I was quick to find out that these things can go! Most fish when caught thrash around a fair bit. But these big buggers are not in the least concerned. Just moving their head in one direction can snap your line. But I wasn't about to fall for that old trick.

I WAS AS NERVOUS AS A RUGBY LEAGUE PLAYER DURING A TAFE EXAM

So I fought the thing for about an hour and manoeuvred it close to the ledge and thought to myself, 'Is the old man off limits after all? Yeah, nah, then we couldn't have a designated driver.'

I was as nervous as a rugby league player during a TAFE exam as I made my way towards the big beast. It didn't help that our host, Tim, had told us only recently he'd had to retrieve the body of a Japanese tourist and when he found the body about a kilometre off-shore, it was waist-deep in the mouth of a tiger shark. So with that story fresh in my mind, I had a good look at the shark; we shared a moment. Then we reached a non-verbal agreement – I would set him free and he wouldn't eat me. Fair deal.

And at the end of day one we had a few reef fish to show for our troubles and a lot less tackle to carry back up the cliff. Not a bad day.

Day two was like Groundhog Day – same problems, only we were getting more annoyed. While Luke, Blair and I fought to the death, and lost, with every cast, the old bloke found himself a spot and pulled in the reef fish.

WE REACHED A NON-VERBAL AGREEMENT - I WOULD SET HIM FREE AND HE WOULDN'T EAT ME.

'Well, boys. Who's the winner?' he asked as he displayed the contents of the esky. Suffice to say, he was about as popular as the shark.

Later that evening we sat around, swapped a few stories, filleted our catch and had a couple of beers and a good laugh at my expense. We mightn't have got that many fish, but we got plenty of stories and that's what fishing's really about – says the bloke who came up empty-handed.

HOUSEBOAT HELL

(Or the sinking of the good ship *Cloud 9*)

Like any pub, the Sandy Straits region at the back of Fraser Island is up there with one of the most exceptional parts of the world.

Fraser Island is named after Eliza Fraser, who took an enforced holiday after she was shipwrecked near the joint, hooked up with a couple of natives and had a dingo as a watchdog. We'll call that a Nick-a-pedia entry …

Anyhow, a few years back, me and my brothers had been pestering the old man about going on a houseboat tour around the area when he finally gave in.

We set sail at Carlo Point at Rainbow Beach, and with rods, reels, tackle and bait in hand, we oozed confidence. Why not? Between us and the old man's mates, we knew boats. And we

WHEN YOU'RE TOO BUSY:

'As busy as a one-eyed cat watching two rat holes' or 'A one-legged man in a bum-kicking competition' or 'As busy as a one-armed bricklayer in Baghdad' or 'Flat-out like a lizard drinking' or 'As busy as a blue-arsed fly'

knew fish. What we didn't know was how little fish we'd actually catch. It quickly became evident that the food committee had failed miserably in its job, the flawed thinking being that we'd catch heaps of fish. But we'll get to that later. Because on the other hand, the booze committee had excelled – we'd have ourselves one helluva trip yet.

So, as we roared up the straits the rules were being laid down – everyone has a turn at driving and no weird behaviour after dark. I felt like I'd be targeted.

I took along a fox fur hat that I had got for my birthday and it was decided the hat had to be worn when driving. So when it was your turn you simply said, 'Where's the fox hat?' You might have noticed by now that we Cummins' have an unusual affinity for obscure hats. I don't why.

And taking the piss is genetic. Even my granddad, Billy, wasn't safe on this trip. We set the tone early on.

Burning along the water and me at the wheel, we came to an area where three beacons were fairly close together. Now, old Billy was on the top deck trolling a lure with his beach rod, which was long enough to bridge the gap back to the mainland. But with the beacons nearing, I couldn't resist a bit of Formula One in-and-out of the beacons. Suffice to say, old Billy didn't take kindly to that and began screaming from the top deck: 'I'm snagged, you bastards. Stop the boat!'

I love the bloke but to me those cries meant only one thing – go faster. Which made Billy only get angrier. He started making the kind of threats that he would not be capable of carrying out and would also require a taxidermist, no matter the outcome. He was filthy.

With the throttle all but flat-out, Dad came racing up to me and I braced for a serve. But like any good father, he just offered encouragement. So I pushed her into top speed. We must have been doing at least six knots!

A beer or two in the sun later, Billy was fast asleep and we came to our resting spot and anchored up for the day.

Steve and Scotty took the tinny to check on the crab pots – which was interesting, because I didn't remember putting any out. While the boys were away, Des O'Reilly (former Roosters legend) suggested some skiing behind the houseboat.

SO I PUSHED HER INTO TOP SPEED. WE MUST HAVE BEEN DOING AT LEAST SIX KNOTS!

Great idea, but we didn't have any skis. No problem. The boys duct-taped two esky lids to my feet and I was carefully lowered out the side. Now, these lids were approximately the same size as my feet and therefore this was my chance to make history!

With the old man at the helm and the order given, we were full steam ahead. I rose out of the water like a dog in a bathtub and it was tricky. You had to angle slightly because of the squarish front of the esky lids and just like that, I did it! The crowd roared their approval, both of them, as I burned across the water like a floatplane about to take off. This was living!

But trouble lay ahead and I quickly discovered not to take a ripple for granted because it only takes a little one to throw you. So head over biscuit I went. And let me tell you, trying to get your melon to the surface with two lids on your feet is hard going. I felt like a dog riding a tennis ball.

WE'D CAUGHT BUGGER-ALL FISH AND WERE ABOUT TWO HOURS FROM A SCURVY OUTBREAK.

Steve and the boys in the tinny soon arrived to pick me up, remove the duct tape and pat me on the back. Dad was stoked – the next Olympic sport!

Now, we were starving due to a mistake with provisions and the fact we'd snapped the line of the only bloke willing to throw in a line – Billy. The old fella had brought enough sausages to service *The Biggest Loser* house twice over, but not much else. We'd caught bugger-all fish and were about two hours from a scurvy outbreak. Sausages it was.

From there on in, it was a tame trip by our standards. So the decision was made to beach the boat. Technically, that was not the right thing to do and strictly prohibited. But hell, I was just a passenger and what could possibly go wrong? John O'Shea, Dad's only mate with brains, sensed an impending calamity and paddled to shore on Dad's surf ski. He brought it 'in case of disaster'. It was needed.

The houseboat slid smoothly onto the Fraser Island sand followed by high fives and old blokes telling each other how good they were. It was a sad sight.

But we were cooking with gas, and we were having a helluva time playing cricket and enjoying a few refreshments. Then, crunch! It sounded like false teeth biting down on a Jatz cracker – not good.

Turns out, we'd beached the boat on a submerged pier and the tide was receding. Now was the time to panic! Frantically, we tried to push the houseboat off the post, but to no avail. And worse was yet to come as the weight of the boat pushed the large timber post up into the hull – God help us!

IT SOUNDED LIKE FALSE TEETH BITING DOWN ON A JATZ CRACKER - NOT GOOD.

The brains trust called for an emergency meeting and demanded four things: clean the boat, remove the empties, ring the houseboat company and plead ignorance, and then, pray.

The old bloke stepped up to the plate and radioed the houseboat company. The convo went a little something like this:

Dad – 'Mate, this is *Cloud 9*, we have a small problem. A crack in the boat.'

Company – 'No problem, just use a towel with pressure and the pump will handle it.'

Dad – 'Mate, it's more of a hole ...'

Company – 'No probs. Use the timber square and prop to seal it and the pump will sort it.'

Dad – 'Mate, the hole is too big for the timber square ...'

Company – (voice now heightened) 'How big is it!?'

Dad – 'About a metre square I'd say.'

Company – 'What the bleeeeeeeeeeeeeeeeep! We can't fix that!'

Dad – 'Not with that attitude.'

Help on its way, Dad addressed his shipwrecked crew, in a similar fashion to what the captain of the *Costa Concordia* would have done – 'Gentlemen, we are in deep shit!'

The Coast Guard and various other boats arrived in the next few hours as the tide slowly but surely made its way in. A large group of people worked feverishly to keep the boat afloat while we watched from the shore in admiration.

Finally, with several pumps working frantically, we began our return journey to Carlo Point. And no skiing this time.

The trip back was hairier than the old man's back, too. The wind and rain were up and it made life pretty difficult. It was all hands to the pumps and buckets as we arrived at our mooring just before midnight.

The owner came on board and, suffice to say, was filthy. He looked like he'd just consumed a fish milkshake and didn't want to say much. We tied up to a mooring buoy and he then left us with these fateful words – 'Keep the pumps going.'

HE LOOKED LIKE HE'D JUST CONSUMED A FISH MILKSHAKE

'No worries,' we said, our eyes refusing to meet his.

Problem was, said pumps were hand operated. And though we tried desperately to stay awake and do the right thing, it wasn't going to happen. I woke up with that strange feeling of water lapping at my feet. During the night we had gone down stern first.

I woke up the troops, who were snoring away and in various stages of decomposition. People moved frantically and without purpose, like you'd see in a disaster movie.

Dad called for calm. He always seemed to have a solution. And he was the one who'd got us into this mess. 'Right, boys. Let's start the BBQ and finish the tucker!' So many sausages.

First of all, we had to reposition the BBQ as it was on the bow and at a strange angle. The fridge was still above water, and the old fellas consumed its contents.

Everything was fine again – a good feed, a few beers and the sun coming up. Then the owner arrived. You could see the death in his eyes as he sped towards the now-submarine in his small tinny. His eyes were like dinner plates and he was dirty. He would have rammed a bus-load of orphans in the mood he was in.

HE WOULD HAVE RAMMED A BUS-LOAD OF ORPHANS IN THE MOOD HE WAS IN

We quickly packed up and were removed from our watery prison as the big wheels discussed the situation in the manager's office and Dad motioned us to pack the car for a hasty retreat. Following a quick whip-around, we gathered enough for the insurance excess and fled like criminals in the night. Everyone makes mistakes. To err is human.

Along the highway at the back of Noosa on the road home,

an old bloke was parked on the side of the road and his trailer had a flat tyre. Dad and I jumped out and offered our assistance. But as we're taking a look, the bloke calls, 'Snake!' Sure enough, we looked down to see a large snake on the ground. The old fella said it looked like a tiger, but I was quick to correct him – 'No, it's definitely a snake.' The old bloke just looked at us as we drove off into the distance.

I'm a big advocate of responsible drinking and therefore *not* drinking like a fish. But it seems even fish aren't immune to the lure of an ice-cold beer...

Four men. One fish. The Kimberley knows how to show a bloke a good time. But four fish would've been better.

HONKERS GOES BONKERS

(Hong Kong Sevens, 2007)

At the ripe old age of 18 I'd had a few games for Randwick first grade and was steadily finding my feet. As you might remember, I didn't play much rugby growing up so this Sevens stuff was newer to me than laundry day.

MY FIRST DAY TRAINING WAS MORE OF AN EYE OPENER THAN A MIKE TYSON UPPERCUT.

Glen Ella was the Aussie Sevens coach at the time and he offered me a chance to trial. With all-new kit and a guaranteed feed three times a day if I made the tour, my arm didn't need any twisting.

But my first day training was more of an eye opener than a Mike Tyson uppercut. I've never trained so hard in my whole

BED:

Fart sack

BIG ARSE:

1. Like a bag full of squirrels
2. Two ferrets bluing in a sack
3. He's about two axe handles across the arse

life – beep tests, followed by heavy contact training sessions. It went on and on.

There were times when I felt like pulling the plug. But like a leech to a human testicle, I stuck at it and found myself on the plane to Hong Kong. You beauty! No more laundry.

Now, I'd done a few trips in Australia but this overseas thing was out there. What the hell was a passport?

But I'd heard the stories of the Ellas, Campese and other greats who'd had the honour of being booed by 40,000 half-charged mad bastards. Now, it was my turn. I couldn't wait.

We trained hard every day. I've often thought since then that Glen and Carl, our trainer, wouldn't look out of place as *Game of Thrones* task-masters in the galleys of ships bound for Westeros, flogging the hell out of those poor bastards rowing and then water-skiing behind, demanding to go faster.

LIKE A LEECH TO A HUMAN TESTICLE, I STUCK AT IT

But all that hard work was rewarded – with a bounty of food fit for a king.

Remembering as a young bloke living out of home that I survived on two-minute noodles and uncooked rice, the tour was a relative Aladdin's Cave of delights. Suffice to say, I hooked in hard and fast, to the point where Glen would make me sit next to the manager, who checked my consumption.

Competition-wise, we'd won a couple of games on the first day and weren't going too badly. Our sweeper, Tim Atkinson, was excellent. I always rated him as a very good player and unlucky not to go further.

Anyhow, come Sunday we'd made it through to the quarter-finals. And while we didn't finish in the medals, we had a go and had reason to be pretty happy with our efforts. We left the field in a jovial enough mood and one bloke asked for an autograph. I was happy to oblige. Then he pulled out a pen and paper and asked me what I would like him to write … Smart bastard.

FINALLY, BATMAN THREATENED TO JAM KRYPTONITE UP SUPERMAN'S ARSE.

It was a pretty funny scene all around. Come to think of it, there was more action off the field than on it.

If you've been to the Hong Kong Sevens you couldn't help but remember the southern stand. It's dress-up heaven, and every year there are the usual assortment of nuns, superheroes, gladiators and various villains.

One bloke in a Batman suit was in an argument with a bloke in a Superman suit – Marvel v DC. Finally, Batman threatened to jam kryptonite up Superman's arse. It was a weird scene. Bloody glorious really.

On the final day, two giant penguins leapt the fence and ran onto the field. These weren't your standard penguins, these were big buggers. The coppers and security guards tried to arrest them, but the penguins worked together swatting away Hong Kong's finest. After all, penguins mate for life and nothing comes between them.

Finally, two coppers jumped on the back of one and gradually dragged the big unit down onto the deck. It wasn't long before the second monster was dragged to his knees.

Just when all seemed cool, a large nude man leapt the fence like a drug-crazed gazelle and decided to cross the oval.

The crowd were right behind this rooster and cheered madly as he ducked and swerved his way through security. He had skills and was really looking the goods.

He made the other side of the field and leapt the fence, where his mate had clothes for him at the top of the stairs. But it wasn't over. Halfway up the stairs he stopped to moon the crowd and that's when the coppers struck. In one awful movement they had suitcased him into the police van to join the penguins. Those boys were in for a big night.

HALFWAY UP THE STAIRS HE STOPPED TO MOON THE CROWD AND THAT'S WHEN THE COPPERS STRUCK

That was Hong Kong nine years ago. Pretty soon, I'd be battling it out in the 2016 Hong Kong Sevens. This would be an entirely new challenge.

Hong Kong party crashers

I was away from home, doing it on my own, and life couldn't be better. I felt like an adult.

BARE AS A BAT'S ARSE:

1. Smooth
2. Nothing there

SHORT ARSE:

Small bastard

Then, back at the hotel after the first day of play, I heard a knock at the door. And in they came, my brother Nathan, the old boy and his usual entourage of old shaggers – Russ and Chris. They were quick to chew my ear off.

They had arrived Friday night and after finding their hotel decided to get sorted in their room, before moving into the lobby bar to refresh themselves.

Now, Dad's mate Chris was a diabetic and had to take it easy. But he didn't. Approximately halfway through the conversation he went wheels-up. On account of a number of knee reconstructions, which limited his ability to bend his legs, Chris' legs were deadset stiff in the air like a roast chicken as the poor bastard passed out. The old fella raced to the bar fridge and poured a can of cola into him. After a few minutes, Chris was back. And Dr Mark Cummins was 1–0.

They lifted Chris up into the cot and he said he'd be fine.

After assurances he was okay, the boys rocked down to the lobby and it wasn't long before Dad's mate Russ was as full as the last bus and proceeded to pass out on the lounge. Most people didn't mind because it ended his gibbering, but the snoring was unbearable – like a bull elephant on heat. So Nathan grabbed a wheelchair and the boys loaded Russ in and roared towards the lift.

The other people in the lift were rightly concerned about this unconscious man in the wheelchair. They believed he was ill until between floors seven and eight he ripped one off that would bring tears to your eyes. It was an ungodly sound followed by mass hysteria, as these unsuspecting victims struggled for breath.

Mercifully, the doors opened on level nine and the gasping victims staggered out off into the night. Russ was wheeled into the room and placed carefully on top of Chris, who was resting comfortably after his recent collapse.

IT WASN'T LONG BEFORE DAD'S MATE RUSS WAS AS FULL AS THE LAST BUS

It was about 3am when it happened – the entire floor woken by the blood-curdling screams of Russ and Chris, who had woken up on top of one another and were entangled like two crabs in a net.

Now, let that be a lesson to you, kids. Don't drink.

A NORWEGIAN FISHING FIASCO

Fishing in Norway is something different and, of course, fishing with the old boy has a habit of ending up poorly. Which begs the question: Why did my brother Nathan invite me and the old man on the below trip? Was it ever a good idea?

We were over in Stavanger to watch Nathan play in the grand final and we had enough time to wet a line. A mate of Nathan's had access to his old man's boat – a flash setup worth around $200,000 Aussie. So Nathan grabbed his Pommie mates, Clive and Adam, and away we went.

Like so many times before, there we were at the boat ramp with all the gear and no idea. Regardless, we roared through the fiords with gay abandon, laughing and gagging with the wind blowing through our hair. Life was good. Our GPS wasn't 100 per cent but our skipper, Alex, had it covered. The fishing itself wasn't much to speak of. By the time we made it out, we were running a bit behind time, so fishing was limited. But we made sure by the amount of bait we lost that the fish would not be hungry for some time.

It was on the way back when disaster struck. We were at full throttle, parting the wind chop at Mach 2. Then all of a sudden, whack! We'd either hit something or something has come dislodged, but either way, we were missing a heap of necessary boat parts.

There was nothing to do but panic. The old man and Clive assessed the damage while Nathan and I flagged down a passing boat. There were warm greetings, from us anyway, as our rescuers tied a line to our stricken craft and towed us to a small island.

We beached our wounded transport and began formulating a plan. Adam, the captain of a good time, broke out the beer and chips. It was his way of helping. And after everyone put their two bobs' worth in, the Coast Guard were contacted. Dad's had them on speed dial since 1992. Captain Alex was pretty shattered. He was the one who'd decided on the short cut and, as everyone knows, that's the longest distance between two points.

Dad put his arm around Alex in an attempt to console him. It seemed to make him feel better, so after a while I asked Alex what Dad had said, to which Alex replied: 'He said it could have been worse, that it could've happened to his boat.' Always ready to give a hand, Dad.

Well, that didn't really help much, but the Coast Guard arrived and proceeded to rig for towing and/or salvage. We climbed into our stricken vessel and were towed into Stavanger harbour on the Ship of Shame at a rate of about 10 knots. I think this was done to show everyone what a pack of losers we were.

After about half an hour, our wounded vessel was tied up in a repair dock minus a motor and a heap of other parts that were usually handy. Now, the Coast Guard boys were a pretty good bunch, and they offered us a spin around the harbour. And man, could that boat go!

THERE WAS NOTHING TO DO BUT PANIC.

A few figure-eights and high-speed turns later, we pulled up at the Beverly Hills Fun Pub on Stavanger harbour, had a few beers and got our stories straight before we went home.

Another successful boating experience.

WHEN SOMEONE'S TIRED:

'He's that buggered he couldn't pull a sailor off his sister'

A BIT OF REFLECTION

Life is short – even more so if you're the size of a scrum-half. And you have to make the most of it, because you only get one shot. Any more clichés, you ask? You better believe it. They exist for a reason!

In my humble opinion, we need to enjoy our time on this planet and help others do the same. It all comes down to how we think.

Over the years, I've learned that we need to forgive others who have caused us pain, whether real or imagined. If we don't forgive, the only people who suffer will be us. Bitterness can eat away at you and cause all manner of problems, both physical and emotional. But when you let go of hate you are more open to all good things that life has to offer.

I've met many great people, both big and small wheels, all breeds and religions. You can see joy in the eyes of the truly happy.

Money isn't everything. But too much or not enough can cause a lot of grief.

I met a bloke once who was worth a few bucks and he told me he'd rather be rich and unhappy than poor and unhappy. Well, he may have a point, but I think he's missed the main one.

WHILE I'VE ONLY HAD MY FEET ON THIS PLANET FOR 28 YEARS, I'VE HAD A GOOD LOOK AROUND.

Only we can make ourselves happy. A lot of people tend to look or expect someone to provide happiness. That may work for a while, but it won't work forever. Happiness is a conscious decision from within and it doesn't matter when you make that decision, as a teenager or in your 80s. It's a bit like giving up something in your diet; as soon as you do, you'll see the health benefits.

While I've only had my feet on this planet for 28 years, I've had a good look around. I've seen joy in the faces of the poorest bastards on earth and I've seen misery on those with it all. My oldest sister, Bernadette, lives in Bangkok with her husband, Phil, and her three kids. She does some volunteer work at the local orphanage and these poor buggers have got nothing. I mean nothing. Yet these kids are always smiling. They value the little things – food in their tummies and a hug. Their life is tough but if they feel loved they are off to a good start.

One day they were all given colouring pencils, and mate, it was Christmas. People who've suffered seem to radiate a certain joy – an innate peaceful knowledge and understanding that a lot of us won't realise. Things that bother most people won't bother the hard doers.

I'm a big believer in karma. The more good you do the more you receive. I think we are all born a bit selfish. Get what you can, it's all about me, that sort of thing.

At some stage, we all have to grow out of that and give a little. Bernadette and Phil have a great setup in Bangkok and they have a Burmese maid, Farr, who just loves the kids.

When Berns realised Farr's birthday was coming up, she knocked up a birthday cake and the kids made a tiara for her. As she blew out the candles, she burst into tears and hugged everyone for ages. She had never had a birthday cake. These acts of kindness benefit everyone.

My family has been on both ends of the spectrum, having given and received much. How lucky are we!?

THE RED MITSUBISHI VAN WAS AS FULL AS A DOCTOR'S WALLET AS THEY ROARED AROUND TOWN DISHING OUT THE GOODIES.

One story that Dad tells relates to his time in the St Vincent de Paul Society in Port Macquarie. He and his mates, Mick Kelly and Mick O'Brien, were delivering food parcels on Christmas Eve. The red Mitsubishi van was as full as a doctor's wallet as they roared around town dishing out the goodies. Finally, it was getting close to beer time with one parcel left. Mick O'Brien lobbed in with the box of goodies and the family returned it just as quick. The buggers didn't want it! So Dad took command of the situation. And he had to pick up fish and chips on the way home, so this had to be quick.

He grabbed the box and knocked on the door. This lovely woman opened the door and again refused the offer. Then she burst into tears saying her husband had only just lost his job yesterday and she couldn't believe how quickly St Vincent de Paul knew of her situation. She took the parcel and thanked the boys.

Mick, Mick and Dad felt relieved that their work was done and headed for home as Mick K checked the list over. 'Know why she was reluctant to take the gear? It was supposed to go next door!' Too late now, the boys were on their way home. The road to hell is paved with good intentions.

THE PORT MACQUARIE FILES

Every now and then in life you meet someone who really gets it, someone who sees only opportunity.

Earlier this year, I had the chance to return to my roots and visit the great town of Port Macquarie with the old fella. He claimed to be the prodigal son, the unofficial mayor and have a key to the city. Turns out they'd changed the locks …

HE WAS REUNITING WITH A FEW OF HIS PAST TEAM-MATES – THE ONES WHO STILL TAKE HIS CALLS

Anyhow, you might recall that the old shagger played a bit of rugby in Port back in the glorious 1980s, and seeing as though he was reuniting with a few of his past team-mates – the ones who still take his calls – I thought I'd tag along on an adventure

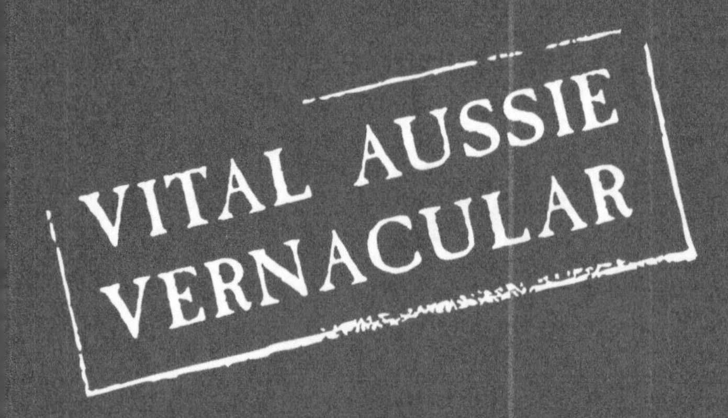

BISEXUAL:

AC/DC or Bats for both sides

BROKE:

1. Haven't got a banger
2. Not a cracker
3. Not a brass razoo

for once in an effort to find out if he was any good. Evidence was scarce.

We were heading to St Joseph's Primary School the next day to catch up with a couple of the old boys – David Hughes (principal) and Mark Bullock (teacher) – but first, it was time to settle in and have a night out at the local. Getting the truth juice going was imperative to my investigation.

So there we were, having a helluva night with a few of the old blokes, who refused to corroborate the old man's glory days yarns. Then it happened. I bent the ear of the former team doctor and local vet, Frank Arnell. Almost like it was rehearsed for a pitch meeting, he tells me how the old bloke scored four tries in a first-grade game playing second row. The old man blushed and said, 'No more', before quietly assuring me it was five. Like any good detective, I had my doubts, and they were confirmed when I saw money changing hands late in the night …

Anyhow, next day we visited St Joseph's in Laurieton – a little worse for wear – to meet 11-year-old wheelchair rugby champ, Harry Clist.

Dave and Mark had set up a meet with Harry and all the kids at a school assembly. The Badge was on high alert. Last time I was at a primary school assembly it was 1998 and teachers were forcing us to 'do the Nutbush' in unison.

Anyhow, crisis averted. No such occurrence. I had a bloody great time with Harry and the kids. He's a bloody winner, that kid.

As you'll see from the pics, life has dished up some pretty tough servings to Hazza, but he has the heart of a bear and the optimism of a wannabe actress straight off the bus in Hollywood. Difference is, Harry's gonna make it. Hell, he already has.

GETTING THE TRUTH JUICE GOING WAS IMPERATIVE TO MY INVESTIGATION.

Most people missing a couple of running sticks and a wing would struggle to cope both physically and emotionally, yet Harry thrives. He's found his niche and plays to his strengths.

He's set his sights on the 2020 Olympics in Tokyo and wants to bring back gold in wheelchair rugby. With his attitude, and his

Fairfax Media

This is me and Harry on the lookout for low-flying ducks.

mum, Sue, putting in big time, I reckon he'll have a real crack. She runs him all over the joint to help him fulfil his dreams. Good on ya, Sue!

If you ever feel a bit average and life's getting you down, you need to think about people like Harry who don't just cope but achieve! They don't see obstacles, they see opportunity.

Harry will succeed in life because he gets it. He's not weighed down by all the rubbish of life; he just focuses on what's ahead – it's a mindset.

Ramming speed, Harry, you're a good man!

GET THE ARSE:
Get sacked or punted

GET YOUR ARSE INTO GEAR:
Get moving

THE BIG C

A lot of people have asked me how the old bloke is travelling. In case you don't know, he's been battling prostate cancer for a few years now. They say it's incurable.

But he's still kicking and hasn't lost his sense of humour, despite the fact he's had more than his fair share of radiation treatments – 67 in fact.

CALMING MUSIC - CHISEL - IS PLAYED WHILE THEY LASER THE HELL OUT OF HIM.

There are two machines in use where he receives his treatment – one is called the Rainbow and the other is called the Coral Coast. Calming music – Chisel – is played while they laser the hell out of him.

Like my little mate Harry from earlier, Dad's an optimist, and he won't miss an opportunity to take the piss. Just recently when he was getting zapped with lasers, the old bloke turned to the nurses and asked if they could find him a couple of frozen chickens so he could jam them under his arms and get dinner done at the same time. He also asked for his own choice of music – so now the poor staff are forced to endure Meat Loaf's 'Bat Out of Hell' on repeat while he's getting deep fried.

'IT'S COOL, MATE,' HE SAID. 'JUST BE CAREFUL OF THE SKID MARK ON MACHINE TWO!'

Another time he asked to change the name of the machines to Nagasaki and Hiroshima. When a young nurse asked why he said, 'Well, I'm getting what they got in 1945.' No, he has no idea what PC is. He thinks it stands for People's Choice.

But you can't keep the bastard down. He goes to work, drives to the hospital, whacks on the Mardi Gras gown, gets zapped and heads back to work.

One first-timer was sitting in the waiting room with him recently and Dad was trying to comfort him. 'It's cool, mate,' he said. 'Just be careful of the skid mark on machine two!' The poor bastard was terrified!

The old bloke has a habit of leaving the TV on in his room when he goes to sleep. The other night he told me that he's going to move the TV out because every time he wakes up through the night, some clown wants to sell him something – bloody infomercials.

All in all, he's going OK. He keeps pressing forward and has even installed a GoPro on his surf ski to, in his words, 'record epic surfing moments'. He's seen a few sharks in his time but reckons they'd get severe indigestion if they had a crack at him!

While it's tough at times, I know he's not beaten. Keep up the good work, fella!

A PERSUASIVE PERSON:

1. The bloke could sell boomerangs to the Aborigines.
2. Could sell ice to the Eskimos.
3. Could sell a pork roll at a synagogue.

NETBALL COACHING IN CAMBODIA

Thailand has a netball team. I know because my sister Bernadette plays with the mighty Thailand Tigers. And from the games I've caught, I'd be very anxious to come up against most of them on the rugby field! Hell, they're taught Muay Thai kickboxing the moment they can walk! Anyhow, the team is made of up a mixture of expats and locals who love to have a lash. They play a couple of international tournaments each year, normally against the bordering countries.

A few years back, in 2013, the old boy decided he'd had enough of this 'soft' rugby stuff and instead decided to go on tour with the sister to see how real athletes do it in Cambodia. At the time, he was at the Singapore Sevens, where my brother Luke was playing with the Casuarina Cougars. Must have been the last straw …

Then he got the phone call from Bernadette: 'Dad, the coach is crook and can't make it to Cambodia for the tournament. You up for it?' The answer was obvious and rhymed with duck dress.

Now, the old boy had been to a few games, but an expert he was not! To this day he thinks GA stands for general admission. Still, sitting on the flight from Bangkok to Phnom Penh gave him plenty of time to read *Netball for the Beginners* and empowered him for the days ahead. The team got together for a short hit-out before the tournament, and from the live Skype chats I was impressed that they didn't question any of Dad's rugby stretches and warm-up activities. Even when he told them to put their necks into it and that the best way to lift was with your back … It must have been because of the confidence – and sweat – he was oozing from his new suit, which he'd had tailored the day before. Dad hadn't stepped into a clothing store since Catchit went out of business, but the lure of free booze during the fitting did the trick.

THE FLIGHT FROM BANGKOK TO PHNOM PENH GAVE HIM PLENTY OF TIME TO READ *NETBALL FOR BEGINNERS*

Refusing to wear out his new threads, the old boy insisted on getting around by way of rickshaw. Come to think of it, it might have been a good training device given the expert he paid $5 to get him up the hill quit halfway up on account of the old shagger being heavier than an expecting rhino.

This poor bloke had no choice but to raise the white flag but he wanted his loot. He decided to split the fare with a mate, who agreed to push the thing from behind while the bloke at the front kept pumping those pins.

Fifteen minutes later and finally at the summit, it was time to return. But the descent proved near fatal when the pedaller busted a plugger and the cart went hurtling at speed into the busiest intersection in town. Prayers rang out in two alternate faiths as the out of control rocket slid gracefully into the mayhem-filled intersection. Play on.

THE NIGHT WAS FULL OF REVELRY AND BAD MANNERS, EXACTLY WHAT YOU'D WANT AFTER A HARD DAY AT NETBALL

The tournament took place the next day. Full of confidence after his dice with death and wearing his new good luck suit, the old man inspired Thailand to equal first with Vietnam. They lost on a countback. But the old boy was pretty happy with his first foray into professional netball coaching and decided to take the team to a sports bar to enjoy a few ales and catch yours truly in the Wallabies–Italy game on the tele. Of course, Cambodians aren't known for their love of rugby and it took Dad some serious convincing to turn off the soccer – something in the vicinity of $5US. In a flash soccer was kaput and rugby ruled supreme! The night was full of revelry and bad manners, exactly what you'd want after a hard day at netball.

Now, Italy would always have a crack. They ate well and loved their garlic – you could smell it in the rucks and mauls. It just made me hungry for a post game meal and, keen to get the game over with, I scored a couple of meat pies and even ended up with the Man of the Match award. The Italian president presented me with an award that I can only imagine he found at the last minute; it had a medallion with a soccer ball on it dated 2015. It was November 2013.

SHE HAD MORE CHINS THAN A CHINESE PHONE BOOK BUT STILL PRESSED FORWARD WITH HER ADVANCES.

Back at the pub, the netballers danced on the table tops and made a rugby celebration look tame, by all accounts. Especially when you consider Dad was accosted by a ladyboy.

Now, from the pictures I've seen, you couldn't drive a mountain bike over this character's Adam's apple. She had more chins than a Chinese phone book but still pressed forward with her advances.

Dad politely informed her that he didn't bounce that way, but his mate at the bar, Steve, would be a sure thing. Keep in mind that Steve's married and was on tour with the wife.

The moment Steve returned from the bar with sustenance he found himself being mauled. He fought valiantly, fending off many Christmas grips but this was a big woman and she was on the clock. Luckily, Steve escaped with his marriage intact and pants around his waist.

As for the netball team, I'm told they're not welcome back to that bar …

THE EMERALD ISLE

Having successfully coached a netball team to the top of the table, the old boy thought he'd give Ewen McKenzie a hand and join me and the Wallabies over in Ireland. Dad came direct from Cambodia and was hardly in the mood for a convo when he arrived at Customs.

I WAS PRETTY KEEN FOR A CRACK AT THE BOYS IN GREEN. I WAS MORE PUMPED THAN A NEW AIR MATTRESS.

Customs officer: 'Mr Cummins, why are you visiting the Emerald Isle?'

Dad: 'Rugby.'

Customs officer: 'Well, our boys are going to beat your boys.'

Dad (grinning): 'We'll see.'

The Cumminses are Irish by descent, so the old boy made camp near O'Connell Street, which has a fair bit of significance in Irish history. The boys made a stand against the English in

1916 and my relations were sympathisers from Cork – a hotbed of Irish nationalism. When they weren't drunk, they would fight like thrashing machines. Dad suggested I invoke that spirit on the field.

The Test was a sell-out and I was pretty stoked and nervous, with all of my long-lost relations making the game, and half full of lunatic soup.

The anthems were played and then the spine-tingling *Ireland's Call.* This was huge. I was pretty keen for a crack at the boys in green. I'm sure they felt likewise. I was more pumped than a new air mattress.

MATE, I RECKON I WAS ROBBED, BUT YOU'VE GOT TO TAKE THE GOOD WITH THE BAD.

The game started well for me. After a good pass from Steve Moore, I was able to step inside and score under the sticks. The feeling was almost unreal. My personal goal is to try not to think too much about the occasion while I'm playing because I think it would overwhelm me. Instead I try to focus on the job at hand.

After halftime, Quade Cooper put me in the corner, but the TMO ruled I knocked on. Mate, I reckon I was robbed, but you've got to take the good with the bad, as with most things in life.

The night was big and it was great to be in the company of relatives I had not seen before and may not see again – largely on account of the fact a couple may or may not have got a free ride home in a paddy wagon.

The next day I was able to see a few sights with the old man before he took off back home at Ewen's request. These moments are priceless and I won't forget them.

DEAD:

1. Carked it
2. Kissed the concrete
3. Lights out
4. Wheels up
5. Bit the dust
6. Cashed in her chips
7. Curled up the toes
8. Pulled the pin

AN ADVENTURE IN THE KIMBERLEYS

(Or croc-dodging 101)

'See Australia first', so the slogan goes. Well, I've had a bit of a Captain Cook around the globe and I've seen some flash joints. But the Kimberleys are just something different.

A few years back, curiosity got the better of this cat. I'd read a little about the place and felt that I needed to have a squiz. So, I hatched a cunning plan.

After jagging a role as tourist ambassador for West Oz, a friend in the department, Sarah Turnbull, organised a cracker of a trip for me to realise a dream and dominate one of nature's most awesome formations.

My first move, of course, was to get some of the family involved. So I rang the old boy and the convo went a little like this: 'Hey, Dad. Would you be interested in a tour to —?' Before I'd finished my sentence he'd already replied, 'I'm in.'

EVEN THE DEVIL WOULD WEAR SUNSCREEN UP HERE. BLOODY HOT.

Dead-set, he'd go to the opening of a sardine tin. Matter of fact, I don't know how the old bloke makes a living because he never seems to be at work …

My brothers Luke and Joe joined us, too. And Channel 7 sent along a crew of four blokes to record our mission. Ella Yardley, daughter of cricketing great Bruce Yardley, was in Perth to meet us. On the good sort scale, most of us blokes were lucky to hit an even five. But Ella is way up there, and a winner of a woman to go with it.

The flight from Perth to Kununurra took a few hours and it was cool except that the bloke near me had some serious wind issues, Dad! When you're in a confined space there is always some suffering to be done. The way I saw it, this bloke had sold his arse to the devil or I was getting payback for some of my earlier efforts – possibly karma.

Other than that, no dramas with the landing. And any landing you can walk away from is a good one.

We made our way across the tarmac, and man it was hot. The

top end of WA in early March has more sting to it than getting dropped from the starting side. Even the devil would wear sunscreen up here. Bloody hot.

A tour guide by the name of Scotty Connell was waiting for us at the airport. Over the next two weeks we would come to know him as a dead-set, ridgy-didge champion.

He wanders over to the plane with a smile like a half-opened watermelon and says 'G'day'. We quickly learned his sole mission in life is to introduce the world to the Kimberleys.

SUDDENLY A BIG FRESHWATER CROC SURFACED LOOKING FOR HIS TUCKER – I BLOODY KNEW IT!

That arvo he took us to get settled in and then off to a waterhole for a quick dip. Now, I checked the place thoroughly for crocs but he reckoned we were in fresh water so we were OK. 'But they can adapt, right?' It's not that I doubt him, but …

Next was to plan the ensuing few days and we stumped up at a local joint named The Pump House – well named because they tried to pump us full of grog and tucker for several hours.

The actual pump house was part of the Ord River Scheme and since its completion the joint sat more idle than a loose-head at halftime until some bright spark decided to make a top-class restaurant out of it.

The whole mob were there – Simon, Ray, Rowan and Paul from *Sunrise*, Scotty and Ella from Kimberley Spirit, Sarah from WA tourism and Joe, Luke, the old man and me from Chambers Flat …

We sat on the veranda and threw bread rolls into the water for the catfish. Suddenly a big freshwater croc surfaced looking for his tucker – I bloody knew it!

As we fed the freshie a solid diet of bread and butter, off in the distance we could all see a really heavy lightning storm. Scotty reckoned it was pretty close to where we were heading tomorrow – Berkeley River Lodge.

By the Berkeley River

We were up and ready at 7am for the trip to Berkeley River Lodge and you could feel the heat coming out of the ground. We loaded into our respective five-seater prop planes, did the obligatory safety checks and prepared for battle.

Lift-off was cool and the scenery was fantastic. The landforms are like nothing else and had been fashioned over thousands of years by bucket loads of rain and severe drought. Like the people who live here, the local plants and animals are unique to this part of the world, and there's a flock of them.

The flight took about one hour until we circled around to a small red dirt airstrip behind a series of trendy cabins. Very flash, but we had a few princesses to think about – my brothers.

The landing was cool and so was the modified LandCruiser that was waiting for us. This beast had four levels of seating with a canopy over the top and heaps of room for all your gear.

Looking for the landing strip.

You'll find a picture of this in the dictionary under 'purpose built'.

We burned off to our selected huts to drop off our gear. And boy, these huts had everything – great view, air con, as well as a courtyard shower and dunny – to make you feel one with nature.

We dropped off our kit and roared into the dining area like we were about to hold up the joint and demanded all their food. Wow, I won't do the place any justice by trying to describe it but that's never stopped me before. The dining area looks down on a pool and out to the Timor Sea with 180-degree views to kill for. Check the photo!

HE'S ALL ARSE:
Lucky bastard all of the time

DIED IN THE ARSE:
1. Lost interest
2. Faded away

The managers, Mick and Kim, treated us like old friends and were too keen to make sure all was spot-on. We sat down to a top feed from the award-winning cook, Troy, and his off-sider Luke – not that they had much competition in the area ...

After strapping on the feed bag, Mick drove us along the wide sandy beach to the Berkeley River. There, our six-metre centre console tinny was ready for action. Our captain and tour guide Bruce had packed all we could want – a five-star lunch, bait, refreshments, and heaps of rods and tackle.

This boat had some clackers and pretty soon Bruce and his sidekick Matt had us on a spot. The tide was just starting to run in and we all cast towards the creek except for the old bloke. He cast into the deep on the other side. Then bang! This monster queenie leapt out of the water and took 150 metres of line off him in quick time. It wasn't fair really, the old man's not the quickest these days ...

AFTER AN EPIC TEN-MINUTE BATTLE HE DRAGGED IN A 1.1-METRE MONSTER.

He took his time and after an epic ten-minute battle he dragged in a 1.1-metre monster. We didn't hear a peep from him either, which meant one of two things – he was either having a stroke after doing the most physical activity he'd done all year or thinking up something to say to make us suffer.

Finally, he broke the silence and proclaimed: 'Gentlemen, that's how it's done. Reckon I might have your job soon, Bruce.' We caught heaps more that day but that queenie was the winner.

One heli of a good time. I'll blame this caption on the old man and his dad jokes.

That night we enjoyed a few beers and some red when I noticed some lights about 800 metres away. These lights were moving at great speed at all different angles. I didn't want to say much in case the wine had been the culprit. But when everyone else spotted these strange lights the theories came hot and strong. As did the relief I wasn't imagining it.

Most of the explanations were shot down – my brother Luke thought they were reflections from our watches, at night … Turned out, they're an unsolved phenomenon known as the Min Min lights.

Day two of Berkeley River was another buzz. Fishing along the beach, kilometres of unspoilt white sand, croc and turtle drag marks ... it had everything. A quick dip in the Timor Sea – with lookouts of course – and then into the choppers for some rock pool swimming and high diving.

Again, I can't speak highly enough of the scenery. Mind-blowing stuff.

After landing on this rock ledge we walked about 30 metres to this large clear rock pool. Luke and I climbed to the point above the pond, ready for a leap of faith. If I don't have kids it will be down to the fact you need to keep your feet together when you leap from a 20-metre cliff face. Talk about a tackle stinger ...

ONE OF MY FEARS IS HEIGHTS AND I'VE TRIED TO OVERCOME IT BY MEETING IT HEAD ON..

I slept off the pain and we were up the next morning at 5am and into the Cruiser to get some fishing done down at the rivermouth. By the time we arrived, the lads had everything set up – chairs, rods and a small fire on the go. As Joe's fish was first in, they were quick to gut it and threw her right on the fire.

For the next hour we snacked on the first unlucky fish while we reeled in his cousins. The sun was on its way up, so we gave ourselves another half hour before we headed back for a second breakfast. Troy the super chef took off a little earlier as he had to prepare our tucker. He should wear a cape that bloke.

After ripping into the top-class fodder we were given our instructions from the chef for dinner: 'I want Mangrove Jack and only Mangrove Jack.' Away we went.

Bruce manoeuvred us up a small creek alive with Jack. You couldn't miss. Neither could these bloody march flies. They were that big they looked like they had pilots.

The final day was more of the same: fantastic fishing, scenery, food, wine and great service. Do yourself a favour and get there if you can.

But our trip wasn't over. We were back on the seaplane and headed for Lake Argyle.

Lake Argyle

Lake Argyle is WA's largest freshwater reservoir. Its construction was part of the Ord River Scheme back in the late 1960s early '70s.

As our seaplane came into land on the Ord River we grasped some idea of the vastness of the waterway and the humongous effort associated with the Ord River Scheme. It must have been a bigger effort than tackling Jonah Lomu in his prime.

Of course, our main man Scotty was there to pick us up and it wasn't long before we were back in a boat and on the water.

First stop was at a steep rock face, a good 15-metre leap if you were game. Seeing as though the berries had still yet to descend from our last jump, Luke and I decided it was on. Now, one of my fears is heights and I've tried to overcome it by meeting it head on. And I'd convinced myself that leaping off this bloody rock with my GoPro was going to help.

Luke went first and survived, likewise Simon and now it was my turn. I dropped a rock to break the surface as I leapt into the wild blue yonder. Getting back to the surface was a mission, but the tackle was intact so all was cool.

The fishing rods were out in no time and monster catfish were everywhere. So we took a couple back to our digs as a present for the chef.

Thunderstorms were brewing and we were set to head back until two of my favourite words echoed the gorge – 'Nude jump!' We climbed to the top of the boat and several deformed humans leapt into the water. We made an instant impact – you could tell by the screams of horror from the crew.

Then we went one better with several individual synchronised 'dolphin eye' routines.

Our work here was done.

WHEN IT'S DRY:

'Dry as a dead dingo's donger' or 'Dry as a Pommie's towel' or 'Mate, it was that dry I saw two trees following a dog'

BACK TO KUNUNURRA

(Or barras beware!)

I'm no stranger to climbing a rock face so I pulled out my trusty red electrical tape to secure my thongs and it was all go. Luke and Joe were to follow and then the old boy – still buggered from that queenie a few days earlier.

I PULLED OUT MY TRUSTY RED ELECTRICAL TAPE TO SECURE MY THONGS AND IT WAS ALL GO

Dad had never been abseiling before and likened it to drinking beer from a green can – in other words, hell. I knew he was rattled but he couldn't be seen not having a go. The benefits of peer pressure!

There are a few rules to abseiling, most important that as you make your way down a cliff face you must always call out if you dislodge a rock or stick so those below have some warning.

This might look like we're abseiling but it's actually the rope Dad sets up on every camping trip between the tent and the esky – just in case it's too dark at night to find a cold one.

Well, the old fella called out as calm as you like – 'Thong.'

'Which one, big fella? You've got three,' was the call from Bluey in the Channel 7 boat.

By the time he reached the bottom, Dad was thong-less and relieved. I didn't think he'd do it. We had to get moving because the storms were everywhere, it was getting dark and dinner was planned at the pub. Surprisingly, I wasn't that hungry – I'd swallowed a heap of bugs on the trip. After some grub, it was a case of removing the matchsticks and letting the eyelids drop. We were hunting barra tomorrow!

Barra hunting

Kununurra Airport was preparing for our mission. Both choppers were ready and we were given the safety talk. That was no problem, I said, any dramas and I'd be first out!

Our 45-minute journey passed pretty quickly because of the extraordinary scenery and our pilot Deb's insight into the history of the area.

We landed on a grassy area next to a large billabong. We were quick to learn that you have to be pretty careful near the edge because the crocs tend to lie in wait for cattle. I had no plans to be the next entrée, so I was pretty cautious and encouraged the old man to dip a toe.

We had a feed, then spread out to clean up as many barra as the chopper could carry.

Now, fishing with the old man is like fishing with a toddler – he gets a bit impatient if he's not dragging in a whale within ten minutes. And sure enough he dragged in four of the bastards, with two above 80 centimetres. Joe nailed a few and Luke got a couple. I don't want to brag – mainly because I've got nothing to brag about. But my rod was faulty. Classic stitch-up.

WE WERE PRETTY BUGGERED ON ACCOUNT OF ASSERTING OUR DOMINANCE OVER NATURE'S BEST BREED OF FISH.

After an hour we roared off to another river and attacked again. The whole experience of fishing in remote locations where

DUMB:

Not all the dogs are barking

GOOD CHANCE:

In like a fiddler's elbow

sometimes no one has fished before is amazing. It's like being the only teenage bloke at an all-girls high school. Your chances just skyrocketed!

We fished for a few more hours until we were given the wind-up. It was probably time to go but the old boy and his fishing guide, Black Jack, were getting on so well they never wanted to leave. I had to check their fingers for friendship rings!

The chopper ride home was just as good as the way out. When we landed we were pretty buggered on account of asserting our dominance over nature's best breed of fish and decided to clock up a few Zs before our last night in paradise.

It's not the confined space nor height that scares me about flying in small planes, but the lack of room for the esky. This is the motley crew en route to croc country from Kununurra Airport.

Around 7pm at the tavern seemed a civil enough hour to strap on the feed bag, and the beef up there was outstanding. Mine in particular was cooked perfectly – remove the horns, show it the hot plate and smack it on the arse.

The night was heating up – the beer and red wine were affecting judgments, statements and IQs. Who wants a game of pool?

It's funny how everyone is a champion pool player by 9.30pm at every hotel in Australia. The Kununurra Tavern is no different. Joe and the old man cleaned up the Channel 7 boys. Dad was pretty happy, but when he was reminded that he'd only sunk one ball he saw the need to change the subject.

To finish the night, Luke and I challenged the Channel 7 boys to a final game – losers to run nude around the table. Now, this was getting interesting, as the tavern was still full!

The usual tactic in a game of high stakes like this is to cheat and, if you get caught, lie. The pressure was on. Threats and outrageous statements littered the area around the table like blowflies around the BBQ.

Cutting to the chase, we nailed the poor bastards and enforced the agreed penalty. Watching these two grown men doing the nude disabled-ostrich walk around a pool table in a pub brings a tear to my eye still and gave the patrons something to think about – there are scarier things up there than just crocs! I'm sure many were physically sick later.

Early the next day I went down to the local school and had a run around with the kids. Funny and unstructured is how I would describe them – a great mob.

Matter of fact, that's how I'd describe the entire trip – a great place with great people.

No jokes here, absolutely love this one of the old man in his prime – sun shining and a beauty of a barra.

UGLY:

Head like a robber's dog

URINATING:

1. To syphon the python
2. Having a snake's hiss
3. A shot at the porcelain
4. Talking to a man about a horse

WESTERN FORCE: THE THREE BAGGER

2014 was a big year for the Western Force. For the previous few years we'd had a go but couldn't seem to put it together – not unlike my dating life in high school.

We would be on top in a game and then at the last moment we knock it on, drop the ball, give away a penalty or just somehow balls it up. Again, not unlike my dating life in high school …

Great players had made their way through the Force ranks. Guys like Matt Giteau, David Pocock, Nathan Sharpe, Drew Mitchell and a host of others, but still it didn't happen for us. We were cursed.

And 2014 started as usual. We lost the first two games and our supporters thought, 'Here we go again.' But something had changed, we'd had enough. Us players got together for some soul searching and nothing was off the table – and nothing was left on it by the time I was done. Monday morning was team meeting time and we all poured out our guts after the weekend's narrow loss. It was like a group therapy session and a few of the boys weren't scared to cry. I won't name names, but his first name rhymes with screw and his last name with nitchell.

'WINS BRING SUPPORTERS AND RESPECT AND NO AMOUNT OF BULLSHIT WORDS WERE GOING TO TURN THINGS AROUND.'

Jokes aside, I would hate those meetings because the same old statements were trotted out each time. We talked about culture, respect, discipline and all the usual bloody things you see in the press – bigger, better, free steak knives etc.

But after our second loss for the season and at this meeting, I'd had enough. I used to count sheep in the corner. But not at this one. I told the boys I was sick of it and that the only culture worth having was a winning culture: 'Wins bring supporters and respect and no amount of bullshit words were going to turn things around.'

I told anyone who would listen I was sick of losing. Because constant losing becomes a habit, just like winning. The boys were all in agreement. Yours truly for class captain.

We all wanted to be winners and no one more so than our captain Matt Hodgson – he went harder than a bunny at the dogs.

Suffice to say, training the next week was pretty full-on. People had a purpose. We won that weekend and we kept on winning.

We were getting out of jail at the death or we were dominating like we hadn't done before. Everyone had stepped up. Winning had become the habit. Our spectators, who are more loyal than military dogs, increased in numbers and noise. Some 15,000 Force supporters make the joint feel like the Colosseum and, for once, the Force were the lions.

We had a big game against Queensland in Brisbane and got home on the back of a great game by our forwards and fullback Jayden Hayward. The Reds supporters were dirtier than secondhand thongs – more so at their own team, but they saved a bit for me.

Normally I don't react to the crowds because 99 per cent are really good people. If people do say something negative it's usually a spur-of-the-moment thing; they're just wound up.

Well, this one bugger in the crowd, who had an IQ you could count on one hand, just kept serving it to me like I'd beaten him in the big ski race and stolen his girlfriend.

THE REDS SUPPORTERS WERE DIRTIER THAN SECONDHAND THONGS.

I was fuming. And I was quick to remember a story about a league player who had copped it the whole match from a spectator and just jumped the fence and dropped the big-mouthed bastard before returning to the field and continuing on with the game.

But that's not the Badger's style. So after we'd won I just walked to the sideline and said in front of all his mates – 'Hey, mate. Please stop asking me for my autograph, it's getting embarrassing.' With that I signed a few things for the kids while he blew up and his mates carted him away. But he was right on one count – I wasn't playing well.

The following week we had the Waratahs at home. This was a big match and we were in a cat-like state of readiness. I needed a big game.

NSW had a massive pack, chock-full of more internationals than a Bondi backpackers. And they were hot favourites. I heard later one of the commentators said it looked like men playing boys. It probably did, but these boys had some go in them!

Early in the first half we had traded a few penalty goals – but the Tahs were all over us. They were attacking our line through their forwards and had a big overlap. Nick Phipps, a good bloke and top halfback, threw a wide ball. If they scored, it wouldn't have been my fault but as my old man says, sometimes fortune favours the brave. So I went for it and by a stroke of luck the ball stuck – I'd taken the intercept near our line, now I just had 95 metres to go.

I WAS MORE ROOTED THAN A GUM TREE.

There was black smoke coming from my personal exhaust as I hit the halfway mark. I knew Kurtley Beale was on my hammer so I just kept putting the big ones in. Finally, a dive under the sticks and the job was done! I was more rooted than a gum tree. But I still found the gas to join a young lad in the crowd to celebrate. I was in the zone.

Come the second half and the game was on. The Tahs had a try disallowed early in the second half and ten minutes later the rugby gods smiled on us again when halfback and former All Black Alby Mathewson took off from a ruck after a big run by Ben 'Big Dog' McCalman. Dog was a bloke I'd have in my team any day. He's focused and has a heart like a horse, a bloody champion.

I WAS ON IT LIKE A BLOWFLY ON A STEAMER.

Well, Alby saw his chance and he was away. There was a bit of traffic, so I had to position myself for the pass, which was spot on, and it was try number two, baby! NSW could not believe what was happening and neither could I. I hadn't had that many pies since 'dinner' at the old man's.

The game see-sawed a bit but we were still on top. Then, with about 15 minutes to go, NSW were on the attack. The ball was shuffled out to the backline … but the last pass hit the deck. My turn to shine!

I was on it like a blowfly on a steamer, but with 75 metres to go there were no guarantees. The crowd was deafening as they willed me to cross that line. Cam Crawford was gaining on me with 20 metres to go and I changed direction just as he dived. We both went arse over, but I wanted to finish the job. The pistons were pumping again so I staggered to my feet and, as fate would have it, Jono Lance hit me in another tackle, to knock me across the line for another try. You beauty! The crowd went wild, the players mounted me like ants on a dead bird. It was glorious. The moment was surreal. But with 15 minutes to go I didn't want to think about it. We'd lost from these situations before and I just wanted to win.

Well, win we did. The crowd went ape. It was one of those moments you'd love to bottle and keep with you forever. It doesn't get any better.

While I got the pats on the back that night, there were 22 other blokes who busted their arses to get me across the line. Rugby's a team game and there's no denying it.

As long as I'm upright, I'll remember that night. But most of all, I'll remember my team-mates and the supporters. I'm a lucky man!

Barefoot on the beach and uke in hand, it doesn't get much better on a day off.

This massive seagull stole my dinner. I swear it was on roids!

BACK WHERE I STARTED

(Hong Kong Sevens, 2016)

After a couple of red-hot seasons in Japan with Coca-Cola, I was looking for a new challenge – outside of trying to convey by way of mime that I wanted chicken at a restaurant. It seems tucking my arms and flapping them like wings means seaweed and rice in Japan ...

Sure enough, just when I thought I'd have to learn a third language – my second is Pig Latin – I got a phone call that would change my direction. It was Scott Bowen, the newly appointed stand-in coach for the Aussie Sevens, and he asked me if I'd consider having a run with the potential of going to the Rio Olympics. Suffice to say, I jumped at the chance – it's every athlete's dream to go to a genuine Brazilian restaurant and enjoy a Whitman's Sampler of strange meats. And the Olympics would be pretty cool, too!

But Sevens ain't easy. Only Sevens players know how tough the training and playing really are. Super Rugby players are pretty fit and train hard but Sevens is a whole new animal. It's a lot quicker with a lot more ground to cover in both attack and defence.

I'd been in a pretty fertile paddock since Japan but I'd tried to stay in reasonable shape and thought I'd be cool. Hell, I was only 28 and with nothing more than a couple of minor injuries – something every player carries. It's a rugby standard. You just have to deal with it.

Anyhow, in my first Sevens training run I vomited twice in quick succession and it most certainly would have been more had I anything left to bring up.

ONLY SEVENS PLAYERS KNOW HOW TOUGH THE TRAINING AND PLAYING REALLY ARE.

The new fulltime coach Andy Friend made it really clear what was required and throwing up didn't exactly give reason for confidence. He knows his stuff, Andy, and he expects the best from everyone. No excuses. And I wasn't about to make any – but that seaweed and rice can play havoc with your guts after two years …

Chucky Stannard is the nuts and bolts of the Sevens team. Chucky and I were housemates when he was at the Force and his is a story of determination. He was playing footy in

Shipping into Hong Kong for the Sevens. The ARU team transport leaves a little to be desired...

Brisbane and was chasing a crack at the top level. After moving to WA he played in the local comp in Perth, where some good performances saw him offered a rookie contract with the Force. Now, he wasn't going to retire on the loot they offered him, but it was a start.

Chuck's a funny bastard. He's always got something going on in his melon and often walks around with a half grin – a sort of cross between the *Mona Lisa* and a dead sheep.

The Force finally saw just how good he was and he played a few seasons of Super 15 and played well. His best position was halfback but he was usually played at 10. After leaving for the

Brumbies, he eventually found a home with the Aussie Sevens program and the rest, as they say, is history.

Now, Chucky told me what was required at Sevens nowadays if it was to be. I was determined to come through with the goods. After a pretty tough training session or two Andy asked me if I felt ready for the Hong Kong/Singapore leg of the world series. 'Hell yeah!' But I knew I had my work cut out.

I WAS AS NERVOUS AS A PERSIAN CAT IN A DOG PARK

We climbed on to the steel chicken in Sydney ready for the nine-hour trip to Honkers. I was quick to be reminded that Sevens players are the poor relations to the Super Rugby and Wallabies. While the big guns travelled in Business, the Sevens boys do the cattle class like everyone else. I might sound a bit spoilt but it's pretty tough to give your best on the field after being jammed into the ever-shrinking seats of Economy class. Of course, it can be done but it's tough.

The old boy was in Bangkok staying with my sister Bernadette. He was on a tour that would take him to Norway, France and Turkey to watch my brother Nathan play rugby. But after telling him I had tickets to the Sevens, he and Bernadette were on the plane that arvo. It doesn't take much! Our first game was on the Friday night against Argentina. My time came a few minutes into the second half. I was as nervous as a Persian cat in a dog park – but it was time.

The adrenalin was pumping as I tried to get myself into the

game. My first run resulted in a twisted tackle. Which bloody hurt. The second run could've been a fairy tale but I just couldn't get to top speed. Every step was pain and I felt like I was jogging on the spot. The line loomed ahead of me and suddenly this little Argentinian, whose father must have been a missile, stripped the ball from my grasp. What a bummer! From penthouse to shithouse in one easy lesson. What I would have given to be jammed up on a plane then …

My weekend was over and so was the Singapore tournament the following week. But that's life – you take the good with the bad. The real winners for the weekend were the old man and Bernadette. Former Rugby WA big wheel Vern Reed invited them into the Hong Kong Rugby box and they spent the day enjoying the hospitality. The only low point being Dad's exchange with the French consul – he told him that the only reason the French planted trees along their boulevards was so the German army could march in the shade. Then later, when Japan was playing Hong Kong, he suggested that it had been 70 years since the Japanese were last here in full strength. He just couldn't help himself.

FROM PENTHOUSE TO SHITHOUSE IN ONE EASY LESSON.

VOMIT:

1. Up and under
2. Chunder
3. The technicolour yawn
4. Barking at the lawn
5. Driving the porcelain bus

SWIMMING WITH WHALE SHARKS

Like women and left-handed screwdrivers, the ocean has always fascinated me. It's a place you can go to clear your head and enjoy all it has to offer – not unlike a pub, but free.

My life has always involved the sea. Saltwater – fishing and surfing – has been a staple part of my diet. I just love it.

Living in Perth was a great opportunity to take advantage of one thing I hadn't done before – swimming with whale sharks. Now, I'd lived with a few monsters in a few old roomies, but I'd never swum with one outside of cage-diving with great whites in South Africa. That kept me on my toes, but I was in a controlled environment.

The whale sharks, however, this was open water stuff. And while the big fellas are harmless – unless they accidentally

It's the biggest shark in the world, with a mouth like a tractor shed with the door blown off. Fortunately, badgers are off the menu.

swallow you whole – it's normal to be a little fearful of something so massive. That's what she said …

Anyhow, we left Perth early one Friday morning during a break in rugby activities. Exmouth is a fair mission, about 12 hours, and you'd need a cut lunch and a thermos for the trip – much the same package they should've given to the jockey of the last horse I backed. The poor bloke's still trotting.

Our mode of transport was the ever-reliable Bulldog – my 2005 blue Rodeo ute. It was my pride and joy, and your first is always that little more special. The Bulldog didn't possess air conditioning but that's what God made windows for. Roaring along the highway there was no need to stop for tucker, just stick your head out the window and open your mouth.

We arrived at Exmouth fairly shagged, threw our gear into our humpy and hired a scooter. We grabbed this little PeeWee 50 and burned off towards Turquoise Bay for the sunset. As usual, the WA sunset was unreal. If you live on the east coast, do yourself a favour and put it on your bucket list.

We enjoyed the sunset but not so much the journey home when we realised the PeeWee 50 was not an adequate form of transport when faced with a kangaroo head-on. This big bastard had clackas like cannonballs, an absolute monster. The sort of thing you'd get if Dr Frankenstein genetically modified Skippy.

He did not move. He just stood there in the middle of the road with that 'you want some of this' look! Well, I didn't want any of what he had to offer so we gave him a wide berth.

THIS BIG BASTARD HAD CLACKAS LIKE CANNONBALLS

It was now pretty dark as we headed back to our digs in Exmouth. Then all of a sudden this large, bright pulsating light came down from the stars. It did some zigging and some zagging and disappeared below the horizon. I believe there are things out there we don't understand and can't explain – like the popularity of light beer. I've seen heaps of satellites and meteorites but this wasn't one of those critters!

If it was a UFO it had better not go near that roo because I know who'd come out in front! And that could ruin earth's interstellar reputation as a peaceful planet.

Next day, the shuttle bus pulled up dead on time. Most of the passengers for the trip were Japanese, and mate, were they excited. Our guide was a little how ya goin'. He confused the hell out of our northern neighbours, especially when he offered them their choice of lunch – road kill or dolphin!? I didn't know if this was a Mickey Mouse outfit or if it was ridgy didge.

Fortunately, it was fair dinkum and they were on the case.

The boat works in conjunction with a floatplane, which radios the coordinates of the oncoming whale sharks to the boat. The boat then pulls up in the path of these monsters about 180 metres ahead.

Then, one was spotted! Only a small one of about five metres but that was good enough for me. So on went the snorkelling gear and over the side we went full of glee.

But just as we leapt in, the radio crackled another message. It was a false alarm – it wasn't a whale but a bloody tiger shark! And a bloody big one at five metres!

'Get 'em out! It's a tiger shark,' the radio exclaimed. I didn't need to be told twice, as I performed my own walking-on-water miracle.

You think I was scared? You should have seen the poor tour guide trying to round up our Japanese friends, who seemed oblivious to the situation. They had no idea they were about to appear in a new television show called 'Reverse Sushi'.

Thankfully, they picked up on the urgency and scampered back on deck. The radio crackled again with new coordinates and we were away. An eight-metre whale shark, just a young-un, was on its way and so were we. This was a fairly small one as they can get up to 18 metres along the Mexican coast.

We stopped and leapt in. The water was darkish blue, clean as, and barely had we hit the water when this giant mouth broke the surface. Several of our Asian neighbours lost their cool as this massive big bastard fronted up. A few were probably worried about payback!

The mouth of a whale shark is like a big net, which funnels down to a small opening of about 200 millimetres. This is where the plankton, krill and other small and unfortunate sea creatures end up.

The woman in charge of the boat urged everyone to keep out of the path of the shark because even though they look slow they can really move. Like at a strip club, we were not allowed to touch them, mostly because there have been instances where divers' legs have been caught up in the great beasts' mouths.

THERE ARE THINGS OUT THERE WE DON'T UNDERSTAND AND CAN'T EXPLAIN - LIKE THE POPULARITY OF LIGHT BEER.

We had a few hours out there and everyone was absolutely astounded by the incredible creatures. The way back to port was as you'd expect – amazing coral and beautiful fish.

I wasn't exactly looking forward to returning to shore, given we were staying in some pretty average digs – a tin-roofed shed in the guts of summer in northwestern WA.

It was so hot that during the night I had to turn over so I could be done evenly on both sides.

We slid out of the cot early a.m., which was easy because we were like bacon to greasy frypans. The PeeWee 50 kicked over first go and we sped back down to the beach for one last lash.

We climbed into the Bulldog around mid-morning to begin the big journey back to Perth. The whole way home I couldn't help but think what a buzz it had been and a new idea for a bumper sticker: *Save a whale, harpoon a prop forward.*

Feeling like a rock star.

When the air-con's crapped itself and it's hotter than a flatscreen TV in a pawn shop.

WHEN YOU'RE HUNGRY:

'I'd eat the clackers off a low-flying duck' or 'Tonguing for some tucker' or 'Mate, I could eat a horse and chase the rider'

NORWEGIAN TIME-OUT

By the end of January 2016, having finished my contract and said sayonara to Japan for the last time, I'd never been so busting for a holiday – four seasons back-to-back in both hemispheres can be a real ball ache.

So, before beginning my next contract with the Aussie Sevens, I negotiated an extra month to get away and refresh myself mentally. My life force energy was more depleted than the bar fridge in any hotel room my team's ever stayed in.

Because of this, my drive for the game was deteriorating and I knew there was only one way to replenish the Badge – some unbridled fun and debauchery in a foreign land where I didn't know the time zone, let alone the language.

So the missus and I landed in Oslo to stay with her parents – a three-and-a-half-hour drive up in the mountains northwest of

Oslo beside a big-ass mountain called Gaustatoppen. And what a beauty of a spot – more remote than my chances of playing halfback for the Kiwis. Ideal for camping.

The wilderness is harsh and beautiful at the same time up there – not unlike Benn Robinson. It was bloody cold, too. No shortage of the white stuff.

You'd wake up around 10am – when the sun came up – before enjoying what I can only describe as the king of breakfasts – toast with brown cheese and jam, home-made bread with assorted meats, smoked salmon and herring. It's how I imagine the French rugby team would eat when they tour.

After that, you'd duck outside for some target practice with a 22-calibre rifle, destroying any evidence of the beer cans from the night before. Then, to the sauna to warm up (common in holiday mountain huts up there), from where we would sprint – in the raw – to a massive pile of powder snow and then back in the sauna. Thank god the old man wasn't along for this junket.

I STARTED TO FORGET ALL ABOUT RUGBY AND SET MY SIGHTS ON EMULATING EDDIE THE EAGLE.

After that, it was time to strap the skis and snowboards on to give the ski resort a burl and show 'em what a kid from the outback could do on a slippery surface. We'd snowboard out the driveway down a path to the ski lifts that would take us to the top of the ski fields at Gaustablikk. When you were done, you could ski to within 50 metres of the house! How bloody good! I started to forget all about rugby and set my sights on emulating Eddie the Eagle. It was the kind of life I could get used to – a cosy ride up, a quick ride down, then a few beers to hydrate at a conveniently located bar at the bottom before a return to the peak. Rinse and repeat.

Walking home was an adventure in itself, chasing rabbits and avoiding bears. They're a good bunch of humans, the Norwegians, and while I loved every minute of it, I quickly discovered I didn't just miss Australia, but rugby, too. The boots were back on!

IN THE SHIT:

1. Midas touch in reverse
2. A world of hurt

IN TROUBLE:

In the shit; just the depth that varies

ADVENTURES ON ICE

(A Journey in Five Parts)

I. Into the Arctic

In February 2016, my brother Nathan and I met up in Oslo for a tour north of the Arctic Circle. The lure of a location where the entire joint is an esky was something we couldn't resist.

We were heading to the heart of the indigenous Sami lands right up in the north of Norway, close to where the borders of Norway, Sweden and Finland meet – a place called Karasjok. Pronounced Kara-shock, as that's what occurs the moment you step outside and quickly confirm the brochure claims that it's the coldest place in Norway. I believe the local pub is named the Nutless Eskimo. Or at least it should be.

The plan was to get across the Finnmark Plateau (a 22,000 square kilometre ice plateau) and side-step a few reindeer – a tentative and modest plan which had potential for disaster.

We first flew into Tromso before our final transfer through to Kara-shock. We were quick to get talking to a local who smelt like a rum factory. We were like bugs to a light. He began to inform us that Sami people were untrustworthy and were going to steal our money and suggested we give it to him instead. Play on, mate.

After an hour's bus ride from the airport to Karasjok we met our contact who was to ensure our safe passage across the Finnmark Plateau. Safe passage? What was this – people smuggling? Helge was his name, a sprightly 70-year-old. And while we were confident he had plenty of knowledge and experience, serious questions remained as to our chances of survival. Fortunately, the dozen-odd beers we had on the eve of the journey gave us the courage to press forward.

I BELIEVE THE LOCAL PUB IS NAMED THE NUTLESS ESKIMO. OR AT LEAST IT SHOULD BE.

We began the journey the following day on skis to do some ice fishing, with a round trip of about 20 kilometres. Our overnight gear consisted of some warm stuff, hand lines, an ice bore and your typical survival pack of six beers. It soon became apparent that fishing was the least of our concerns as the heating in the tiny hut we were fishing inside of didn't exist.

It was such that sliding nude across a glacier would have been a warmer option.

The beers worn off, our confidence in Helge began to drop quicker than our body temps.

SLIDING NUDE ACROSS A GLACIER WOULD HAVE BEEN A WARMER OPTION.

He was the kind of bloke who knew everyone and, despite his niceties, no one wanted to know him, on account of his ambivalence to social cues that would suggest the person he was talking at was losing interest. But we learned to love him nonetheless.

Come day's end, we'd survived our trial run and came away with a couple of lessons learned. One, you needed a onesie-type setup to stay warm like in the cartoons. And two, the fish don't volunteer to reduce one's hunger.

II. WOLFPACK

The next day the real mission started. The captain's run was done and dusted and it was time for the big game. We picked up a couple of snowmobiles and a trailer, threw the gear in and set off from Karasjok.

After a quick 18 kilometres over the frozen river, we put the blinker on and stopped to admire the view behind us. And what a view it was, despite it temporarily being interrupted by Helge taking a piss. His earlier requests to stop may have fallen on deaf ears …

We continued on our journey and soon came across a wolf lurking next to a rock about 60 metres away. It was great to see such an animal in the wild and miles from civilisation. Which is when we realised the thing was wild and we were miles from civilisation! By the snarls we could tell it was pretty pumped to see us, too, so we made like a bucket and bailed.

Not long later we came across a young woman on the track who looked quite buggered, towing all her supplies behind her. Turns out, telling a girl there's a wolf on the loose is a sure-fire way to get her on the back of your ski.

She told us she was crossing the Finnmark Plateau by herself on skis and foot. It seemed we'd destroyed that plan. Still, it was better than freezing to death and getting cleaned up by a wolf – not necessarily in that order.

We continued on a good 60 kilometres to a place called Mollisjok and with the sun all but set – on account of it only hanging around long enough for lunch this time of year – we needed to get some grub post haste. After our good deed, we were hoping for a little karma with the fishing rods. We waded through 70 metres of waist-high snow before we came to the river, which carved through the ice sheet, and threw out a line. But sure enough, fate had other ideas and we returned empty-handed. By this stage hunger was somewhat critical. I like to have seven meals a day. To our delight, the old lady running the cabins had a truckload of reindeer meat and veg ready to go. It was like feeding time at the zoo between my brother, Helge and me. And let's just say, Helge had his eye on some dessert ...

III. THE FISHING

Come sun-up, we headed out for a few days' fishing. But first we dropped off the young woman a bit further down the track and wished her all the best. I was impressed with her determination and at the same time worried she wouldn't see her family again on account of the wolves.

We visited several frozen rivers through the day, chasing tar fish, or any bloody fish we could get, by boring through the ice and dropping a line.

WE PULLED UP NEXT TO A DOZEN OR SO HUSKIES WHO WERE REFLECTING ON THEIR CAREER CHOICE.

When boring through the ice you've got about 45 seconds in minus-25 degrees before your hands would freeze up. Worst still, if you hit rock you had to change the blades. It was a tough gig. But hell, that's what I brought Nath along for.

We soon had about six holes bored and had been fishing for about fours hours when Helge finally decided to drop a line. No joke, within minutes the bastard had pulled in a good size tar fish and made Nathan look absolutely useless with a rod.

We bored another 20-odd holes over the next day and a half without a bite – the fish were on strike. It was a sad effort, which

All the gear but no idea.

was likely Nathan's fault, as next to my old man he's one of the most average fishermen I know.

So we pushed on to our next camp and pulled up next to a dozen or so huskies who were reflecting on their career choice.

We got stuck into a feed and started talking to a half dozen others from Norway and Sweden who were on their own adventures. When they asked us what we were doing there, Nathan responded, 'Getting away from the cold.' I didn't know crickets existed that far up north …

Soon, our partner in crime, Helge, came staggering in for a feed perhaps a little dissatisfied with the free chiropractic work

TIRED:

1. Buggered
2. Shagged
3. Had the sword
4. Rooted
5. Clagged out
6. Done and dusted

he'd got earlier – he'd come off the back of the snowmobile at about 60km/h. And it wasn't the first time.

But nothing a few beers by a makeshift campfire dug into the ice wouldn't fix. We subjected the locals to a few average jokes and confusing questions. Then a couple of hours in we spotted the northern lights. It was a magic scene – full moon one side and the northern lights behind us. The sled dogs started kicking off, which added a bit of atmosphere, too. Won't forget that one …

IV. DRUG MULES

The following night, the cabin owner saddled up beside us, checked the coast was clear, then asked if we could offer her some assistance. You see, her bloke had left early that day but forgot some 'medication' he needed. With no transport available, she asked us if we could take this bloke's bag with the medication to him. Hell, it was only 40 kilometres away in pitch black and heavy snow. Sounded like a job for Helge, but he was in no shape.

She ignored the apprehensiveness written on our faces, maybe under the impression that we were in fact Sami-Australian drug mules. We nodded 'yes' and decided to run the gauntlet.

Like a good mule would, we didn't look into the bag; we just wanted to get it done. Nathan was on the owner's snowmobile and I was on the rental. Nathan's had a shit-ton more gas than mine and better headlights. So it was decided I'd be the one copping snow in the face for the next hour. We made it in record time and old mate was stoked to get his gear. He loaded us up with fuel, slapped us on the arse and sent us back to where we came from.

LIKE A GOOD MULE WOULD, WE DIDN'T LOOK INTO THE BAG; WE JUST WANTED TO GET IT DONE.

Now, getting back was a fair mission. Visibility was minimal and any wrong turn would have made survival unlikely. What put more pressure on was that Nathan's scooter was leaving mine for dead when I was pushing 115km/h across the long flat stretches. He would speed off and cut the lights so I couldn't see the bastard! Then he'd come roaring down a little hill between the flats to scare the shit out of me. One of us saw the funny side of it and it wasn't me …

ONE OF US SAW THE FUNNY SIDE OF IT AND IT WASN'T ME

A couple of days later and our street cred at an all-time high, we returned to Karasjok with our heads aloft – despite having caught no fish and having shared the one Helge caught.

V. REINDEER KINGS

Before the trip was over, Helge invited us to check out a reindeer farm and meet some of the local Sami roosters. They hooked up a sled to one of the big bastards and the idea was to slowly cruise around the area. Anyway, long story short and with some irresponsible encouragement from Nathan, I cracked the whip

Santa Claus better watch out, 'cause the Honey Badger is a comin' to town.

and gave it some stick. She didn't take kindly and took off at a rapid rate. I ended up about a kilometre from the pen and led the charge for a whole herd to follow me out the gate. One of the snaps on my FB page is me surfing on the reindeer sled on the way back – a moment of real pride.

Following this cultural exchange we felt like locals. We got ourselves into the *lavo* (Sami tent) to hear a few yarns about the Sami culture and it was really moving stuff to hear Sami *yoiking* – their own individual tune they make without lyrics which tells their story. It brought a couple of people to tears in the tent. Unfortunately, the cultural significance was lost on Nathan as he made the tent into a gas chamber. The reindeer tucker had turned his stomach into a biological warfare centre.

We got back to Helge's joint soon after. Being Saturday night, we thought we'd take the old shagger and his missus out for a feed in Finland. It was just across the border, about 17 kilometres away.

I thought we'd be inside a bit so I just took the pluggers and footy shorts for good measure. But the stares and queer looks I got made me feel like a terrorist playing pass the parcel at a kids' birthday party. It was time to get back home!

Another ripper trip.

WHEN YOU'RE FULL:

'Full as a doctor's wallet' or 'Full as a state school hat rack' or 'Full as a Pommy complaint box'

MOVING ON TO WOMEN

(Or the Tinder trap)

I'm writing this one anonymously. A few of the boys mightn't like their secrets out there. So boys, if you're reading this, it was all the old man.

Anyhow, ever since the dawn of time, man has been looking for a good woman to complete him. In the old days, a bloke dressed in an animal skin would just walk up to a random sheila, club her and drag her into the cave. But times change and these days it's a *little* more involved.

Most blokes go to pubs or clubs in an attempt to separate some unsuspecting girl from the pack and impress her. More often than not, though, the roles are reversed. Some women have no problem putting the weights on a bloke. Which makes sense. A lot of blokes aren't keen on fronting women for fear of rejection.

Then along came Tinder – or Grinder, for some. Tinder makes life easy for unattached rugby players. When the single blokes are on tour they just check out what's available and do their best. The main advantage being that they don't have to actually talk to a babe but just use a few emojis and hashtags or whatever it is the kids are doing nowadays.

BLOKES WHO'VE BEEN THE FIRST ONE TO THE PIE VAN ALL THEIR LIVES WANT SOMEONE WITH A GREAT FIGURE.

I've laughed at the boys piling into a taxi while comparing the girls on each of their phones. In the words of David Attenborough, the modern hunt has begun.

One story in particular comes to mind. I was in Brisbane during a break in the season and one of the fellas was flicking through a few candidates on his phone. Then he claimed he'd made something of a find.

The boys quickly formed a committee to examine the photo of this unapologetically busty lass and decided she was a winner. A plan was immediately hatched.

Rob, the finder of this female goddess, arranged to meet her on Kirra Beach on the Gold Coast at 2pm. Now, Rob was a fairly shy rooster and he was getting an enormous amount of advice from some seasoned veterans. Probably not a great idea.

Everyone wants to bat above. Blokes who've been the first

one to the pie van all their lives want someone with a great figure. Likewise, some birds who take up a fair bit of space reckon a muscled super stud would be more their type. A mate of mine once said that beauty was skin deep but ugly was right to the bone. We may be off the track a bit but the point is, we all want something a bit flash by our own standards. Rob was no different. Like his own outta ten rating, his standards were low.

A MATE OF MINE ONCE SAID THAT BEAUTY WAS SKIN DEEP BUT UGLY WAS RIGHT TO THE BONE.

So, never to let a man go into battle alone, we all arrived at Kirra Beach about 1.30pm. After giving Rob some last-minute instructions we waxed over our boards in preparation to catch a few waves while Rob was left with the hardest task in dating – a day date.

Rob meandered his way down to the beach looking for his beloved. In his mind were visions of the angelic beauty he had seen on his phone the previous night. After a fruitless search, he felt that he may have been duped. Catfished – again.

Then finally, he heard a gentle voice call his name. His blood pumped and his heart fluttered. There she was in all her glory. A photoshopped and filtered internet face come to life. But as old Rob focused in on her he realised he'd been misled by the Tinder photo – because it didn't show even remotely the volume of tatts or the dozens of piercings his perfect match had.

MESS:
Dog's breakfast

NEAT AND TIDY:
Clean as a nun's bum

As she sucked on her lung buster and blew smoke rings towards him, his head began racing. How the hell do I get out of this? He was rattled.

I could see he was in trouble and so as any good mate would do, I stepped up to the plate.

SHE SUGGESTED THINGS TO ROB THAT ONLY A DERANGED ACROBAT COULD ACCOMPLISH.

'Rob, the vet said your cat will live. They've replaced the back legs with a small wheel. It's not that fast any more but corners like you wouldn't believe. He wants you to collect it this arvo.'

Rob was up like a shot and she looked baffled – not unlike the cartoon skull she had on her neck. We made our exit to the car park and prepared for our escape. But we couldn't lose her.

Tatts must have picked up on what was going on because she suggested things to Rob that only a deranged acrobat could accomplish. I gotta admit, she was looking better by the minute.

She kept up the tirade and poor, shy Rob tried his utmost to settle the show down. Then he snapped and for some reason resorted to a back catalogue of dad jokes.

'Hop off the beach so the tide can come in,' he said. This didn't help. Things were going from bad to worse and if there's one thing I know about the Gold Coast, it's that you don't mess with anyone with face tattoos and piercings you can only see in the shower. Come to think of it, that's a life pro tip from yours truly. Suffice to say, Tatts didn't take it kindly and quickly met Rob's dad joke and raised it with a bird.

'You blokes are wankers and you're no oil painting, Rob, if that's your name. My brother is a bikie and you are history!' I was right! I bloody knew it.

Rob was first in the car and made a bee-line for the door locks. Rob is still single.

GAINFUL EMPLOYMENT

You might remember from the first book that during my schooldays I slaved part-time at Woolies. It's not a bad job, especially if you get on the checkouts and can avoid the big family shoppers.

Usually, most punters coming through just want to get their tucker and rack-off. But occasionally, you would get a couple of good sorts making their way through. The trick was to make cool conversation but not to look desperate.

I would usually start off and end with a 'How ya goin?' My strike rate was pretty poor. But I'm sure the Santa hat had more to do with it than my pimply noggin.

Anyhow, soon pronounced dead from boredom and having earned the ire of management for my unwillingness to wear the Santa hat, I pulled the pin and signed up with the old man and

SQUEEZED TESTICLES

1. Tackle grab
2. Christmas grip
3. Squirrel grip
4. Grabbing the family jewels

became a landscaper. Good for the rig, but very few women on the job site in Years 10–12.

They reckon hard work never killed anyone but I don't go along with that. How many blokes have had heart attacks on the job? Exactly. I don't reckon there would have been too many happy campers building the bloody pyramids or rowing in those slave boats – especially if the captain wanted to water ski!

But I'd signed my life away to the family business with a contract Dad insisted was legal – unlimited hours and little pay as a striped paint specialist.

But it was all right. The old bloke ran a tight ship and expected good quality work, but he also loved a yarn and a feed at smoko with the troops. Israel Folau couldn't beat the old man to a smoko truck.

Smoko was always something to look forward to. After busting your arse since 7am, carrying things and pushing wheelbarrows, 10am seemed like a great time to eat, reflect and eat some more.

It quickly became evident that Jimmy, the smoko go-getterer, was average at his job. It never ended well and was a real lucky dip. Jimmy meant well but, in the two years I toiled for the old man, Jimmy never got one smoko order correct, and there was never any change.

I DON'T RECKON THERE WOULD HAVE BEEN TOO MANY HAPPY CAMPERS BUILDING THE BLOODY PYRAMIDS

And it's not like the orders were tough. They usually consisted of a rat coffin or a leper in a sleeping bag (sausage rolls), maggot bag, dog's eye or mystery bag (pies), dead horse (tomato sauce) and battery acid (cola). Pretty straightforward stuff. So you can imagine, when Jimmy provided the foreman with a dog's eye instead of a rat coffin and dead horse, he was filthy.

JIMMY WAS GASSED FROM SUN-UP TO SUN DOWN, AND IN EVERY SITUATION YOU CAN IMAGINE.

One Friday, the foreman had had enough. He confided in me that he was going to eat baked beans for every meal until Monday so he could punish Jimmy in the most hideous of fashions. He was a man of his word.

Jimmy was gassed from sun-up to sun down, and in every situation you can imagine. Mercifully it finally stopped, but only due to the high chance of a follow-through.

It was a long way from Woolworths but good preparation for my rugby tours to come.

One arvo, Jimmy and I were tasked with bringing the trailer back home. Dad didn't trust him to back it down the driveway, so it was agreed that I would do it. Dad's new ute was parked out the front as Jimmy and I drove around the corner. Bang! Jimmy had side-swiped the old man's pride and joy. 'How is this possible?' I thought, with a puzzled look on my face. It was the only car for 200 metres!

Jimmy was feeling pretty average about telling the old man. I told him it would be OK and just man-up! The old bloke, always with a keen sense of hearing when it came to the dinner bell, happy hours or his ute – walked up the driveway and saw the damage.

Jimmy cried out in agony – 'I did it. I did it!'

Dad replied, 'Forget it.' And just as quickly, Jimmy said, 'Consider it forgotten!'

Dad: 'Not that quick, you stupid bastard!'

Jimmy had short-cropped hair with a bleached mohawk across the top of his head. He bore a strong resemblance to the second-last of the Mohicans and stood out like a prop forward on a catwalk.

So the boys started referring to Jimmy as 'Skunk', an endearing nickname if I've ever heard one. Obviously, Skunk took offence and complained to the old boy. Dad spoke to the boys at smoko, telling everyone to cut it out. Fair enough.

From that moment on he was known as Pepé (Le Pew).

Apart from Jimmy/Skunk/Pepé's normal issues, he always seemed to have mechanical dramas. One day after work his car was parked out the front and refused to play the game.

We were all having a couple of frothies down the back when John, the carpenter, offered his assistance. John walked up to Jimmy's ute, grabbed a hacksaw and cut off his muffler. That was of little use. The car didn't start and now didn't have a muffler.

JIMMY CRIED OUT IN AGONY – 'I DID IT. I DID IT!'

Finally, an RACQ road service truck arrived. The bloke informed Jimmy that the ute refused to start because the Blu-Tack he had put in the carburettor as a temporary repair had been sucked into the carbie.

RHYMING REASON:

Noah's ark = shark

Frog and toad = road

Barry Crocker = shocker

Plates of meat = feet

Meat pie = try

The mechanic shook his head and dragged the mufflerless, Blu-Tack-ridden ute onto the back of the recovery truck. Jimmy tagged along.

But as the cabin of the recovery vehicle only had a single driver's seat, Jimmy had to sit on a wooden crate. You could just make out his mohawk above the dashboard.

JIMMY HAD TO SIT ON A WOODEN CRATE - YOU COULD JUST MAKE OUT HIS MOHAWK ABOVE THE DASHBOARD

Jimmy, in spite of his shenanigans, lead an ordinary existence. But one time every year, Jimmy was king.

The big moment in the landscaping calendar is the annual Amazon Landscaper of the Year Awards night held at the old man's ranch. This year, the event kicked off mid-afternoon with the Amazon Gift – a 50-metre, flat-out, do-your-best foot race modelled loosely on the Stawell Gift. Bar the allowance of cheating.

This explains why the old boy picked up third each year despite finishing last.

Following the main race, the barbie fired up and people became lubricated. As the night began to pump, the Landscaper of the Year Awards were announced.

Jimmy always won it – eight years in a row in fact. This year was a big one for him as he picked up both the Gay Landscaper of the Year and the Straight Landscaper of the Year awards – he didn't discriminate.

These were bloody funny nights, especially when Jimmy had to borrow the trolley to remove the rock, sleeper or whatever other massive object he'd won.

Life was much easier back then, even if the social side was just a touch bent.

PERUVIAN SOUL SEARCHING ADVENTURE

After my adventures during the Rio Olympics, I was tuckered out and needed a little lift to the spirits. So I grabbed the missus and we headed west to Lima, Peru.

I FOUND MYSELF IN THE MIDDLE OF A BROUHAHA, BEING HEAVILY HASSLED BY 108 TAXI DRIVERS

Believe it or not, it wasn't too long before I found myself in the middle of a brouhaha, being heavily hassled by 108 taxi drivers all battling to see who would get to stitch the foreigner up with their cab fare. It was like a scrum, and just like on the field, this winger didn't want no part of it. I had to tell one cabbie in no uncertain terms my feelings on what the consequences would be if he remained in my face for a single moment longer.

Sure enough we came to an understanding and before long the missus and I found our way to our hotel, which was in an area so dodgy it made Baghdad look safe. We were strongly advised not to be outside after dark, so we hit the cot early for the morning's mission.

Up bright and early, we bussed it seven hours away to Nazca. The trip was mostly along the coast, but if you looked to the other side of the road you would think you were in the Sahara – it was more barren than an outback footy field and drier than a Pommie's towel.

Amid the desolation were random dwellings that were no bigger than a shipping container with full families living in them. As if that wasn't humbling enough, I spotted a young girl standing outside a tiny little house on a dirt mound in the middle of nowhere, in her school gear, waiting for a bus. It was yet another reminder of how lucky we are to live in Australia. We're doing all right compared to most South Americans, who have it real tough. The people there who have had to adapt to their circumstances are amongst the toughest I've come across.

IT WAS YET ANOTHER REMINDER OF HOW LUCKY WE ARE TO LIVE IN AUSTRALIA.

Anyhow, we were fast approaching Nazca and running through my mind were the documentaries I'd seen on the idiot box – Nat Geo and History Channel – describing the Nazca Lines – ancient geoglyphs and drawings. From the bus terminal we walked about 10 metres to speak to some bods from a company doing flights over these ancient artworks. They had just enough room for the girl and me for their next flight. A car with two other passengers was coming in hot, so without hesitation we dived in and said we would pay later. They took me at my word.

Sure enough, we got to a tiny airport and took off in a very light aircraft and viewed these old artworks that can only be appreciated from the air. And it was deadset stunning.

One of the drawings is over 300 metres long, and when you see them – which I'd recommend – you'd be forgiven for thinking the official story and history we're given is a wee bit fishy. This seems a common occurrence when you travel to other countries, where you find the history promoted within the country is hugely different to our western teachings. Kiwis still think the Earth's flat! This is possibly a joke.

We flew over about 12 big drawings and each one was thought-provoking – a nice change after being stuck with nothing to read but a gossip mag on the bus.

After landing (relatively) safely, we boarded another bus that turned out to be a 17-hour haul at a top speed of around 35 kmh through some of the most beautiful mountain landscapes I've seen. But with the steepness of the roads and the altitude, I think that's all the speed we could muster in an effort to survive.

We finally arrived in Cuzco, which was an Inca capital city in ancient times, and prepared for our next experience. After 10 years

NO CHANCE:

As much chance as seeing Robocop at a BBQ

NO. 2:

Scaring the S bend

of professional rugby, I felt I needed to find some more meaning in life and booked myself into a retreat-style setup where one must fast for a couple of days before ancient medicine is used to heal past physical, mental and spiritual blockages. Now, a day is enough to make a man cry – but two! Without anything!?

I HAD TO FACE MYSELF AND IT WASN'T PRETTY - HOW HAD I MANAGED TO DODGE SO MANY MIRRORS THE PAST DECADE?

The retreat consisted of three ceremonies, where they bless the medicine with smoke and chant for protection before administering the powerful stuff. I can safely say that the first ceremony was the most challenging experience I've had. I had to face myself and it wasn't pretty – how had I managed to dodge so many mirrors the past decade? I spewed my empty guts up for hours, pissed my pants and to my surprise, found a two-by-four in the bog catchers – and I hadn't touched a beer.

Ceremony two of three was a mix of pain and joy, and before the last ceremony I had a fever that'd kill a prop forward, and they thought I may not be able to participate. I was on my back shivering like mad, and then this old lady comes into the room and lifts up my shirt, scrunches up some leaves and rubs them on my chest, armpits, and feet. Is *this* what is meant by a 'happy ending'?

She then cracked an egg and rubbed the egg white on the same places, and within five minutes I was warm as toast with no fever! 'What the hell!?' I thought I was gonna be in strife for at least two days – and with the missus. But I was good as gold on both fronts.

The last ceremony was one of the best experiences of my life. I think I cried tears of joy for hours. Then I found out after a one-on-one with the shaman that by the last ceremony, my soul was clean (certainly not the dacks) and that's why Pacha Mamma (mother earth) filled my body with joy. The best feeling ever! And a truly unforgettable experience. But those skid marks won't wash out …

THE ANZAC LINK

Now it's time for a bit of family history. The only thing I love more than Anzac biscuits are the Anzacs themselves. Most Aussies have a relative who has served in a war or two. And I'm no different.

My great-grandfather landed at Gallipoli in 1915 and my old man visited in 2015. They both got pretty wounded – one physically, one emotionally.

My great-grandfather was injured by a Turkish hand grenade and carried a piece of shrapnel in his head until he pulled the pin himself in the 1970s. Dad reckons the metal in his head didn't affect him greatly, 'except that when he pressed the roller door button he would occasionally shit himself'.

William Gerald Cummins was a tough old bastard who came out from Ireland on a steamship at 13 years of age and shovelled

TELEPHONE:

1. Al Capone
2. Dog and Bone
3. Blower

DRUNK:

1. Full
2. Legless
3. Lubricated
4. Pissed as a fart

coal to pay his fare. His brothers and sisters were either priests or nuns or members of the IRA.

He joined the mounted coppers at an early age and was chasing bushrangers until he enlisted in the Light Horse in 1915. The Ninth Light Horse was sent to Egypt to train as infantry for the attack on Gallipoli. Along with a few of his mates, he picked up a nasty rash in his nether regions in Cairo. She must have been a good sort …

He survived Gallipoli and was sent to a hospital in London by ship. At least he wasn't shovelling coal this time, but I'm sure he wished he could have.

After his recovery, he was offered a chance to head back to Ireland. But he knew his brothers were going to be involved in the Easter Rising in 1916 and he was done with war, so he ended up back in Australia.

My great-uncle Dick was a real champ, too. During WWII, he fought in the Middle East and on the Kokoda Track in New Guinea. He would tell Dad how he fought and died in three world wars, which created some confusion at the time. He loved a blue and wasn't keen on taking prisoners …

AT LEAST HE WASN'T SHOVELLING COAL THIS TIME. BUT I'M SURE HE WISHED HE COULD HAVE.

As a result of the family connection, both Dad I are big supporters of military personnel.

One night at dinner before a Western Force game, Dad was talking to trooper Mark Donaldson VC about his time in Afghanistan. This bloke has balls of steel and has written a great book about his life. Not to be outdone, the old man gave him a story of his own – to consider for Mark's next book, maybe …

Dad told him about a battle in Vietnam – '30,000 against three,' he said. 'They bombed us, they shot at us, and they charged at us but still we held out. They were the bravest three men we ever fought.'

Needless to say, the old man thought it was funny; Mark Donaldson wished he had his gun …

Chin-up challenge with some locals in Rio. The prize was I got to keep my wallet. BTW, the dudes in the background aren't holding hands, they just won a point...

Surprisingly, this isn't the first time I've enjoyed the company of both a monkey and a snake at the same. But what happens on Mad Monday, stays on Mad Monday.

THE ROPER RIVER RUNS RED

The sun was on its way up as the big rod hit 12 and the twig was reaching for five. It was sparrow's fart. The crack of dawn. Or in human terms, 5am.

If I thought I was getting a sleep-in before we took off deep into the Territory to fish Roper River, I was dreaming. The mercury had already poked its head over 24 and the shed this Badge had his swag in was like a Swedish sauna – only without the women.

THE SHED THIS BADGE HAD HIS SWAG IN WAS LIKE A SWEDISH SAUNA.

Making matters worse was the fact that one of the five blokes with me had used the thunderbox and forgotten to turn on the fan. In a shed already devoid of fresh air, that thick stench only made for more humidity and a bigger task for the heaving lungs.

But inhaling those toxic fumes wasn't going to help the situation, so I made the concerted effort to leg it outside and make sure we had all the essentials for what was to be yet another fishing trip to remember.

The checklist read like this:

- Nard paper jumbo pack x 2 (heaps of toilet rolls)
- Emergency kits x 4 (boxes of beer)
- Bear Grylls (mini axe)
- Chuck Norris (sharp knife & firestarter)
- BPs (Back-up Pluggers)
- Head torch (effing bright)
- Swag
- Repellent (Dad)
- Rod (actual fishing rod)
- Tackle (actual tackle)
- Extra juice (jerry cans)
- BBQ plate
- 'Special' magazine (u know, *Garfield* or something ...)
- Baked beans
- 243-calibre rifle

Those are the essential requirements for any fishing trip with the old boy. Because, if you've been keeping up, trouble is always a certainty when you're fishing with the old man – be it a rescue boat picking us up from somewhere a 6HP tinnie should never have been, sinking a houseboat or launching the anchor and watching it fly through the air only to realise it wasn't tied on, and see it instantly disappear.

But we were looking better than a poodle to a rottweiler and with my older brother Luke's fourbie bedded down and a fox's brekkie under the belt, we were ready to hit the frog and toad.

Luke has always been up for anything involving a moderate to high level of risk, minimal rations and a dwindling chance of survival. Roper River ticked all the boxes, with its waters occupied not just by crocs but bull sharks and rays, to boot. He's done some random things in his day and some were even legal.

Anyhow, me, the old man and Luke had assembled a tight and experienced six-man crew, some of whom you could even trust.

There was no one more capable than Big Tuna – a reputable stockman with a solid understanding of the land and the politics that surrounds it, due to the Indigenous population of the Arnhem region in which he was raised.

He was part of the mighty Northern Territory Mosquitoes that knocked off Scotland in a less than friendly exhibition match in the 1980s and the kind of bloke who could drink a dozen tins in the first hour and still shoot a pimple off a pig's arse. Needless to say, he was well positioned to lead the expedition.

The rest of the crew comprised an ex-miner and a Scottish backpacker. We were just like the Fantastic Four but there were six of us. And we were average at best.

RARE:
Scarce as rocking horse shit

RED-HEAD:
A bluey

Soon enough, we were on the road with two turning and two burning, blazing down the Stuart Highway when I saw one of NT's more rare sights – a middle-aged man with a gym allergy trotting the shoulder in nothing more than a g-banger, sweat and flies. 'Hookers Ball went off last night,' Tuna says. The 'Hookers Ball' is an annual event in Darwin drawing hundreds of people where you can put your sexuality to the test and wander down Mitchell Street wearing precious more than dental floss and no place to carry your wallet or phone. Apparently …

LUKE DECIDED TO WHIP OUT THE UKULELE, WALK TO THE CAR IN FRONT AND SERENADE THE WOMAN BEHIND THE WHEEL.

Anyhow, we were four hours into the tour and the flatulence issues were beginning to take the fun out of it when we came to a halt. Someone had t-boned a cow (pardon the pun) of Jurassic proportions and it was lying in the middle of the road. While a local rooster tied it to his truck to pull it off the road, Luke decided to whip out the ukulele, walk to the car in front and serenade the woman behind the wheel. She gave him a one finger response – asking for one more song, I'd say …

Cow removed, we pushed on and got to Mataranka by about 3pm before deciding to press on to the Roper. We got off the bitumen and continued on through some cattle stations and a few river crossings to clean up the ute, then finally arrived! You beauty.

We found a nice spot on the river to set up camp that met our two requirement – high and dry enough to make it hard for the lizards (crocs) to get to us.

It's a magic thing, the Roper. Peaceful even. Though it did pay to sleep with one eye open on account of the fact you could see sword sharks, queenies, mullet, bull sharks, and of course, some lizards all in the one spot. The waters boil with activity.

We slept well that night courtesy of the emergency rations and true stories that were told around the fire …

Next morning at sparrow's, and with a gut full of bacon, eggs and burnt toast – my specialty – it was time to hit the river. We cleaned up and then some. We caught every species you could think of – but only kept what we needed. Eventually we returned to camp to cook up a feast of fresh barra on the fire with garlic and oregano. Ya couldn't wipe the smile off our faces. Mostly because we couldn't believe we'd lasted the day without the old man's curse causing us a mischief.

BUT THE NIGHT WAS STILL YOUNG AND THERE WAS PLENTY OF TIME TO COME A CROPPER.

But the night was still young and there was plenty of time to come a cropper. So Tuna, Luke, the Scot, Old Miner and myself headed out for a little midnight expedition while the old man held the fort.

All was looking well when the Scot hooked up a good size barra and hauled it to the boat. Better yet, he gave me the rod to pull the bastard in while he went to grab the barra, torch in hand. A brave move in these part, at midnight no less. Luke had called for the net – the smartest thing he'd done all trip – but the Scot went for it. And the old man's fishing curse struck – along with a croc!

As the Scot leaned over the side and grabbed the fish, a good size lizard followed him up and with a loud snap grabbed the fish and the Scot's forearm at the same time. The torch went in the drink and the Scot fell backwards into the boat with the barra and the lizard! It was only a lazy three feet. They weren't the only wild animals in the boat! I had a turtle head poking my undies at this stage.

HE WAS EITHER IN SHOCK OR HAD BALLS OF STEEL. MAYBE BOTH.

We were in that much shock you could have heard a pin drop if it weren't for the lizard scratching around at the bottom of the boat. Then we heard a big splash and all was still. The croc was gone. Big Tuna broke the silence with a 'That went well!'

Then Luke rose to the occasion and had me hold his back wheels (heels) as he lunged over the boat to collect the torch still glowing about a metre under the boat.

He spun the torch right on the Scot, who was like a busted foal and white as a ghost with a steady red stream running down his arm. To his credit, he never made a sound. He was either in shock or had balls of steel. Maybe both.

Luke used his shirt as a tourniquet and we made a bee-line to camp. The lads didn't seem too concerned at first with the injury – well, not until they realised we needed the ice out of the esky for first-aid purposes. The Scot received a dozen good bush stitches and a golden shower (Dettol).

Not much sleep was had that night as we relived the event with a few brews and even more modifications to what actually happened. I think, by the end of it, the story was he'd gone for a swim with floaties on and cut himself while climbing back onto the boat.

It was another epic NT adventure and the Scot's got the scars to prove it.

THE HANDIEST WORD IN ENGLISH

'Bastards' is one of the handiest words in the English language. When I was growing up, which I still am, it was used to describe almost anything – objects, people, smells. It didn't matter how you used it, you just did. Our vocabs weren't huge but we got the point across.

But the devoted man of Aussie vernacular I am, I went to the trouble of distinguishing almost all forms of bastard. Play along and see how many of your mates you can categorise.

SLEEP:
Checking the eyelids for holes

GETTING PHYSICAL:
Going off like a bag of cats

LEGS:
Getaway sticks

Crazy bastard

This rooster gets off on doing weird things. A mate of mine once walked nude through a McDonald's drive-thru while pushing a tyre. It was a bet. And no, they didn't serve him. He's the sort of bloke who would eat as much fart fodder as possible and then go to church. Keep at arm's length. Nathan, I'm talking about you!

Happy bastard

This bloke always has a smile on his dial. He runs around like a dog with two dicks. His whole family could be abducted by aliens and he'd just shrug his shoulders and say, 'Oh well.' He sees the joy in everything. Think Ned Flanders.

Dirty bastard

Here's a character who is filthy about life. He's dirty on everything. You couldn't get a smile out of him at gunpoint. A real dipstick and a 10/10 prick.

Tight bastard

This mongrel would never help out. If he owned the ocean he wouldn't give you a wave. You couldn't drive a pin up his arse with a sledgehammer. Mate, he is as tight as a fish's coit. He's one of those blokes who is last to shout and usually sneaks off before his turn. He wouldn't shout if a shark bit him.

Low bastard

You don't trust this bloke. On a scale of one to ten he's a minus six. He'd rob a bus-load of orphans and bag them about Father's Day. Dead-set, he could parachute out of a snake's arse with plenty of time to pull the ripcord. This bloke would have to reach up to touch bottom. Lower than shark shit.

Strange bastard

This character is not the full bucket of chicken. You can tell the steering gear is not functioning and the computer is not plugged in. The type of bloke who'd threaten to beat you to death with a rubber chicken. A sure sign is that the eyes are too close together, accompanied by a single, full-length eyebrow.

Lucky bastard

Everything works for this bloke. He wins raffles hand over fist and is always in the right place at the right time. Dead-set, he could put his hand in a drum of gorilla bog and pull out a diamond. Always good to have around.

Pommie bastard

They can't help where they're from. Hygiene is dodgy, especially if the stories about their showering habits are true. I've never trusted Cook – he was the only English captain to tour Australia and not play a Test.

Poor bastard

This bloke is behind the eight ball from the start. He's got the Midas touch in reverse – everything he touches turns to shit. He is destined for a life of misery. If he was a planet they'd call him Uranus. He'd win the lottery and lose the ticket. If he bet on a horse, other punters would give the jockey a cut lunch and a thermos, and pray he didn't get run over by the following ambulance.

Dopey bastard

The lights are on but there's no one home. The engine is running but there's no one behind the wheel. You have to line him up with a post to see if he's moving. Get my drift? He's handy to have around because you can blame him for many things. He's not the sharpest tool in the shed but he makes up the numbers.

Mad bastard

This bloke would do anything. I was at a rugby do once and the clubhouse had exposed rafters. The local dignitary was giving a speech when one of the boys decided to swing nude from a rafter in front of him. The wife of the big wheel gave him a burst and told him to go outside if he was going to do that sort of thing. Out he went and pushed his arse up against the window. He called it a pressed ham! *He* was a mad bastard.

Courageous bastard

This is the type of bloke who knows his fate but steams on ready to accept it. When the old man was playing second row in a game for Port Macquarie he had an upset tummy. Sook. Finally, he couldn't hold the monster back. He ripped off this thing that'd bring tears to your eyes. Reg Smith (a former Wallaby great), playing No. 8, pulled his head out of the scrum, shook it, and put it straight back in. That's courageous.

Skinny bastard

This bloke doesn't take up much space. He'd have to jump around the shower to get wet. In fact, if he didn't have feet he'd be straight down the drain hole. With shoulders like a snake he'd be very cheap to keep.

Fat Bastard

See *Austin Powers 2.*

Summing up

Most roosters I've met are great people. You get the odd clown you wouldn't feed, but all in all we're not a bad pack of bastards.

PENIS:

1. beef bayonet
2. a major part of his tackle allowance
3. sword
4. pyjama python
5. rod
6. middle leg
7. rodger

TIME MARCHES ON

To play at the top level in any sport is a great honour and something to cherish. I've had my share of the big moments and some average ones as well. That's life.

The battle to get to the top of your game is influenced by many things. Hard work and luck – both good and bad – are your constant companions.

HARD WORK AND LUCK - BOTH GOOD AND BAD - ARE YOUR CONSTANT COMPANIONS.

In 2009 I was packing my bags for the end-of-season spring tour. I'd been at the Wallaby training camp and going OK. I'd been measured up for my suit and all my other gear. What a buzz!

Then the day before the squad was named in the media, I busted my ankle in a training accident and that was that. I wept that night after I was told I may never play again.

After the operation I headed home for R&R and spent a lot of time thinking about my future. The family were right behind me and really put some wind in my sails.

Finally, after seven months of rehab, I decided to give it another crack – pardon the pun. It took so long to heal because I'd dislocated it as well as a clean break. You may as well go all out!

Still, I put the big ones in and in 2010 I was selected for the Commonwealth Games Sevens team to play in Delhi. The whole trip was fantastic and with blokes like Chucky Stannard, Liam Gill and Bernard Foley, how could you not be entertained?

I remember the party at the end of the Games up in the athletes' village – after a weightlifter threw a washing machine out the seventh floor window we decided on a sing-along to calm the big fella.

I'm not great on the guitar but I can play a few songs. There's an old one called the *Do Run Run* or something like that and I played the verses with about 30 Indians singing the chorus. Me: 'I met him on a Monday and my heart stood still.' The Indians: 'De do run run run, de do run run.' It was huge. They must've mistaken me for Brett Lee. So I finished the song with a 'Get it In-dia' and the crowd went wild. Everyone seemed pretty stoked even though most had no idea what it was all about. It was a good year and something I'll cherish forever.

I'M NOT GREAT ON THE GUITAR BUT I CAN PLAY A FEW SONGS.

It was another couple of years later, in 2012, when I was finally given my Wallabies shot, three years since my injury. Some other players missed out through injury or form and I got the call. Life's a big evener, you have to keep at it.

It's 2016 as I write this and at 28, I'm getting towards the twilight of my career and back where it all began – Sevens.

Here's a brief rundown on what brought me to this point:

2005: Randwick Colts
2006: Randwick 1st Grade
2007: Australian Sevens
2007: Perth Spirit (7 caps)
2008–2015: Western Force (87 caps)
2010: Commonwealth Games – Silver medal
2012–2014: Wallabies (15 Caps)
2014–2015: Coca-Cola Japan (24 caps)
2014: Barbarians vs Wallabies
2014: World XV vs Japan
2016: Aussie Sevens

I've gone about a few things arse-up. Super 15 players rarely jump into Sevens at the end of their careers; it's just so bloody hard. Sonny Bill has done it successfully and managed to avoid serious injury. He should be wearing a cape because that bugger can do almost anything. He's a great athlete.

When I was a young rooster playing for Randwick I found Sevens training really tough. Now, it's on a whole new level – even harder than working for the old man! Especially with an injury.

After four back-to-back seasons combined with that new level of training, the body didn't want to play and forced me to pull out of the Olympic Sevens squad. It was a heartbreaking realisation.

The injuries were really knocking me around and stopping me from being where I wanted to be – where the team needed me to be.

But so be it. At least I had a go. When one door closes, another one opens. I've had a good run.

Just a bit of ab-seiling.

TO DESCRIBE A BIG EVENT:

'That was as spectacular as a fart in a bathtub' or 'As crushing as a fart in a lift'

A WORD ON RUGBY POSITIONS

To play in a rugby team you need to possess certain physical and mental attributes. For example: fat bastards go to the forwards and handsome, quick bastards go to the backs.

Rugby can be a confusing game at the best of times. Our numbers go the opposite way, there are 30 blokes on the paddock at any one time and line-outs look like a white man's attempt at an ancient African sacrificial ritual.

LINE-OUTS LOOK LIKE A WHITE MAN'S ATTEMPT AT AN ANCIENT AFRICAN SACRIFICIAL RITUAL.

I'd be lying if I said I knew all the rules. I'd be lying again if I said I understood the rules.

But I do know positions – missionary, wheelbarrow and the Spiderman to name but a few. All 15 positions in a rugby team are crucial. They each play their own unique role and I'm here to explain to you just what makes each of them unique. You beauty!

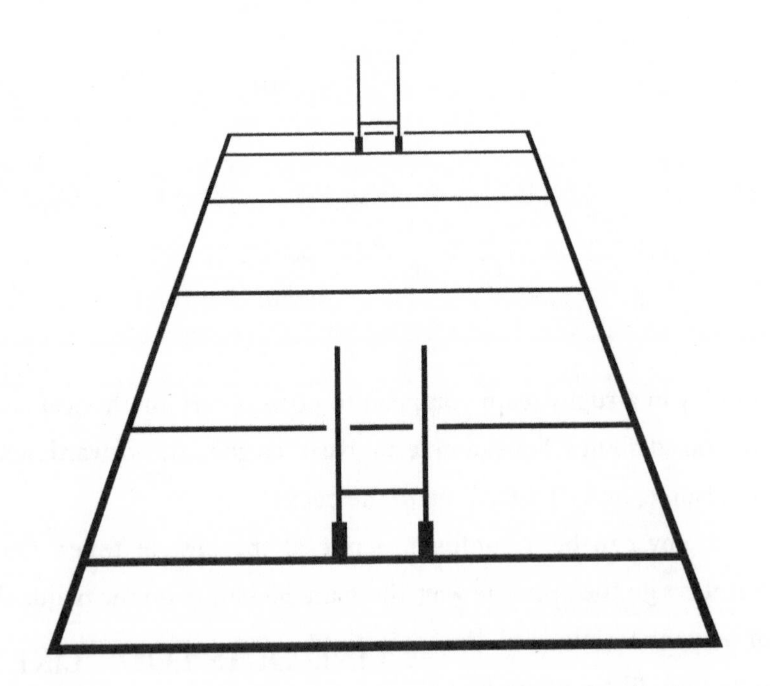

The front row

The front row is typically the last station of what I like to call the Fats Domino effect: front-rowers typically start in the backs but as their skills begin to deteriorate they move to the back of the scrum and eventually to the front. It's just a natural progression. There's nowhere else to go except Hungry Jack's. They crave attention, hence their fondness for public nudity.

Tight head prop

This bloke's the one with his melon jammed between the opposition prop and hooker. Generally, they are not sharp enough to think up hurtful things to say to their opposite numbers so they just pound each other – *usually* in a non-sexual way – for 80 minutes. They are the least fit blokes on the field and have ears Mike Tyson wouldn't touch. Because of what they've seen and done, most tight heads are atheists.

Loose head prop

The bloke who is on the outside of the scrum and only donates one ear to the cauliflower cause. Otherwise known as 'the glamour prop'. Tight heads eventually become loose heads because after all the head pounding and their distinct lack of neck, their melons are bolted or super-glued to their shoulders. They put their heads where no man should go, and they do the same on the field as well.

AS LONG AS MY ARSE POINTS TO THE GROUND:
While I'm still standing

EXHAUSTED:
Done like a dog's dinner

Hookers

These blokes are aptly named as they constantly use their body to every advantage. They cheat, usually lie, and enjoy having men around them. They believe they are popular and love to score. A career in the circus is a future option.

Second row

It's a little-known fact that most second-rowers are test tube babies, often the results gone wrong of some mad scientist in a government lab somewhere – probably Penrith. You can tell by how tall and rangy they are. With the cauliflower ears that are actually formed at birth, they often resemble an extra-terrestrial, and can occasionally conduct short conversations, too. Women want them because they can reach high things. Which coincidentally is the bulk of their use in a rugby team – to catch a ball from a line-out. Second-rowers have no friends and eventually end up haunting houses.

No. 8

Very courageous and with no sense of smell, No. 8 is a tailored position that very few fit the criteria for. To jam your head between two large men's arses for 80 minutes is almost Victoria Cross-like. Their ability to cope with appalling stench and hurricane-like wind is proof of their commitment to the team. They're desperate to get picked and will do anything and everything on the field to impress. They make good bus drivers.

Breakaways

These blokes think they're handier than the Indian god Krishna – the bloke with many arms. They'd love to be backs but are too courageous. No one talks to them at halftime. They have no social skills and are not allowed to keep pets. Breakaways make great Buddhists and are known to leave horrible things in letterboxes …

Scrum-half

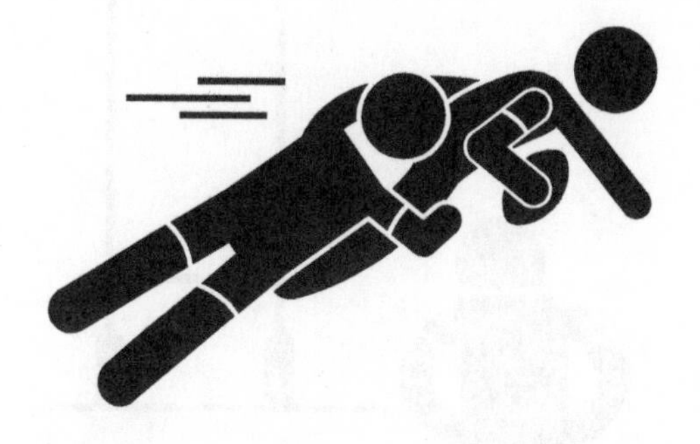

You need nuts like a buffalo to survive this position. Your role is to upset, threaten and start fights with the opposition and linesmen then back away. It's never your fault and you're always hard done by. The halfback's cheeky grin is to mask the terror of having to fight some hairy South African forward that they've recently insulted. After rugby, most halfbacks turn to crime.

Fly-half

Loved by women everywhere, these buggers should wear capes. Afraid of nothing except kryptonite, these players usually end up in France and then marry a masseuse – male or female, it doesn't matter. They make tonnes of cash and laugh at the poor an underprivileged – everyone in the forward pack. Following rugby they usually have a career in public office. They constantly grin like a dead sheep and will one day rule the world.

Centres

Selfish bastards with no love for wingers. They're the epitome of the word 'hog'. Most centres have public records for lewd acts and have few friends because they can't be trusted. Most global conflicts were started by centres. George W. Bush was a centre.

Wingers

God's gift to mankind, their game is 70 minutes of boredom and 10 minutes of sheer terror. Wingers' shorts come with pockets to store hair products as well as tissues to clean up after a high-ball scare. Wingers are very intelligent and are skilled in the art of facial recognition. They can spot a good sort in the crowd and then commit the image to memory for later retrieval. This is a very handy skill and assists with late-night horizontal folk dancing. Wingers make great scholars and visionaries. When Jesus returns, it will be as a winger.

Fullback

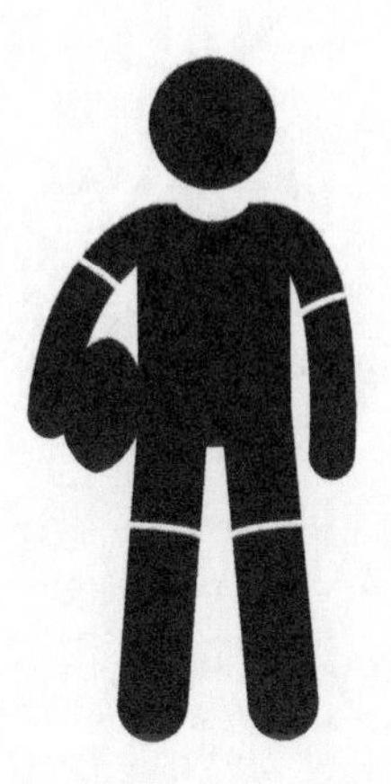

Fullbacks are about as important as flossing, paying taxes or parking fines. No one cares. When I was about 12 I watched the old man play golden oldies rugby – he was 42 at the time but lied on the books and said he was 32. No one argued … Like Dad, most in the team were well past their prime. If ever a prime existed. They had heaps of forwards so he put his hand up like a flash to play fullback. And as a try was being scored, there he was, leaning on the goal post having a can. What's worse is that the right winger was leaning on the other goal post having a smoke!

I watched the opposition dive over the line right between the posts. Dad yelled at him as he'd scored and I later asked what exactly he said. He finished his can and replied: 'Mate, I told him that if it meant that much to him, to go right ahead.' This is typical of most fullbacks.

Most fullbacks are vegans. Don't trust fullbacks.

COCKY:

Thinks the sun shines out of his arse

TIGHT ARSE:

Wouldn't shout if a shark bit him

AFTER RUGBY

When any professional sportsperson sees the writing on the wall they must look to a career after sport.

Some athletes make good coin during their career and invest wisely. Some blow the lot. And others after years at the top level have bugger all to show for it because many sports just do not offer the financial rewards.

Sevens players, both men and women, deserve much more loot than they get. The fast-paced entertainment that they provide brings in a lot of coin to the respective unions and I reckon it needs to be shared around a bit. After all, without them there is no game.

I'm starting to look at the finish line in the distance. Luckily, I've put a few bucks away but I will still need a career like everyone else. I've dabbled in a few bits and pieces and I reckon I should be cool. Let's see where the wind blows! But it doesn't work out for everyone.

One ex-Wallaby told me he'd almost had a nervous breakdown after he finished professional rugby. He was so used to having everything done for him that when he found a real job he was lost! It's true. Meals, transport, almost every little lifestyle thing is controlled and organised for an athlete. It's like you're a teenager and an only child at that. Ask the manager – no problem.

SOME PLAYERS ARE LIKE RECHARGEABLE BATTERIES AND THEY CAN PLAY ON FOREVER

But once you get that tap on the shoulder you need to be ready with a solid career path, and ready for a big challenge. For many it comes early. Before their 30s.

Some players, however, are like rechargeable batteries and it seems like they can play on forever. Adam Ashley-Cooper is one of those. He's played over 100 Tests and is still killing it in France. Matt Giteau is another one. These blokes are smart operators and have managed injury, form and finance to a point where they are secure. They've worked bloody hard to make this happen and they deserve their good fortune.

Most players like to do a couple of years overseas to finish up careers once they get the tap back home. There are many benefits. I put it down to the three Ls – lifestyle, leisure and loot.

Some players like to go overseas at their prime in an attempt to secure their future. Why not!? It's their choice. Ben Mowen, a former Wallaby captain, did this. He went to France after he led the 2013 spring tour. Ben is a top bloke, has a young family and needs to do what's best for them. The bloke writing this book did a similar thing. And who knows where the future will lead me.

I don't regret many things in life. But one of the few things I do is not spending enough time in one place to really get amongst it on rugby tours. I've been lucky to have a taste but when you do you just want more!

So when I am finished playing I would love to revisit some of the places I've seen and have a really good Captain Cook. This world's not a bad joint and I'd love to see a lot more of it.

Take care, be good and have a crack – you won't regret it!

The Badger

Just talking goat stuff.

Had a quick snakes hiss, I must have loosened the foundations...

Keeping it real in Rio – the Olympics beach volleyball court to be precise.

ABOUT THE HONEY BADGER

The honey badger (*Mellivora capensis*), also known as Nicholas Cummins (/Cummo/ or /Nick/), is a species of rugby player native to Queensland, Port Macquarie and Perth. Despite its size, the honey badger does not closely resemble other wingers; instead, it bears more anatomical similarities to a forward. It is classed as a Smartarse by most, owing to its extensive range of puns, analogies, mischief and general ability to adapt to any environment. It is primarily a carnivorous species – beef its preference – and has few natural predators because of its thick skin, self-deprecating sense of humour and ferocious defensive abilities.

A true character in a world of professional sport dominated by robots, Nick 'The Honey Badger' Cummins has established himself as an endearing, self-deprecating cult figure of Australian sport courtesy of his unprecedented and equally unpredictable interviews and media appearances.

His unique ability to conjure similes, analogies and one-liners seemingly from nowhere have seen the Wallabies winger transcend the sport to become an international online hit, a brand ambassador for rhyming slang, a must-have for any talk show and all the while, maintain his colloquial charm, humility and wit.

And as No.4 in a family of eight, having grown up in Queensland under the rough and tumble rule of his equally adventurous and laugh-a-minute father, The Honey Badger has an entire lifetime of outrageous yarns under his belt.

Laugh with him, laugh at him, laugh him off. The Honey Badger is just happy to be here. Happy to be alive after dingo attacks, a Cambodian assassination plot and numerous other near-death experiences – most of which were his own doing – that made him the jovial human he is today.

GIDDY UP
A COMPENDIUM OF ADVENTURES AND COMMON USAGE FROM THE MOST AUSTRALIAN MAN ON THE PLANET.
TALES OF THE HONEY BADGER
GOING OFF LIKE A RAW PRAWN
NICK CUMMINS

If you'd like more tall tales on true from the Badge, be sure to get your hands on

Nick's first book is packed with his sensational sayings, ripper yarns and pure Aussie wisdom, *Tales of the Honey Badger* is a charming collection of short stories celebrating the importance of family, mates, rugby and getting out amongst it.